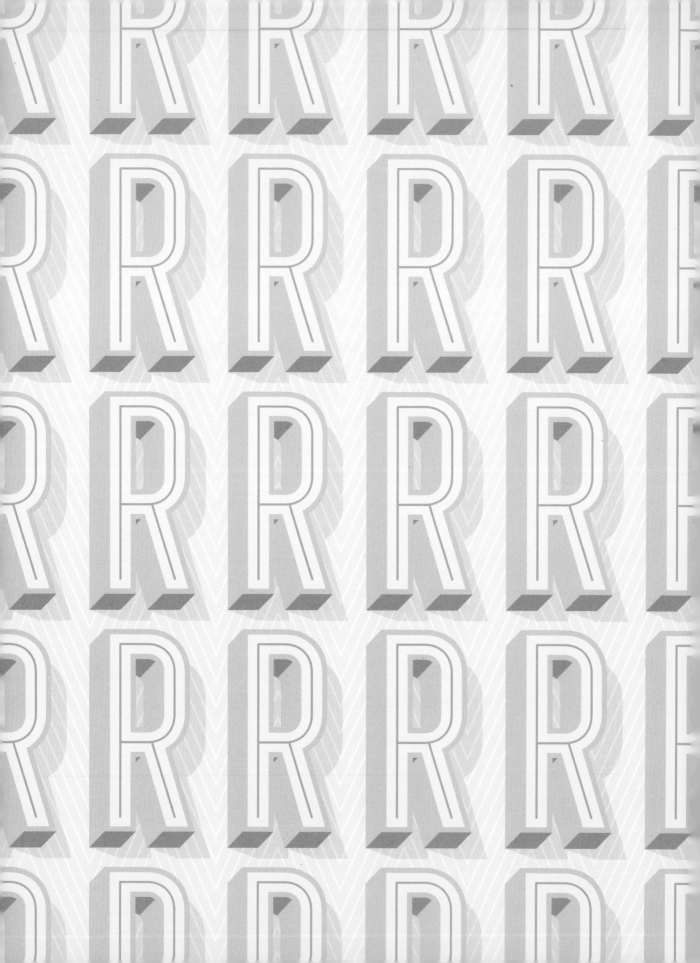

THE
DESSERT
GAME

THE DESSERT GAME

Simple tricks, skill-builders and
show-stoppers to up your game

REYNOLD POERNOMO

Co-founder of KOI Dessert Bar

murdoch books

Sydney | London

CONTENTS

INTRODUCTION 6

CHOOSE YOUR OWN FLAVOUR ADVENTURE 10

PAGES

14 – 65

Brownie 18
Crème Caramel 20
Burnt Honey Basque Cheesecake 22
Chocolate Mousse 26
The Best Basic Butter Cake 30
Matcha & Yuzu Ganache Tart 34
Citrus Meringue Tart 36
Chocolate Choux 40
Individual Pavlovas 44
    Cherry & Coconut Pavlovas 47
    Spiced Apple Pavlovas 48
    Boozy Berry Pavlovas 52
Rum Ba-banana & Pineapple 54
Orange Blossom Ice-cream Sandwich with Lime Curd 58
Vin & Grapes 62

LEVEL 1

TAKING IT EASY

PAGES

66 – 125

Watermelon Jar	70
A Slice of Irish Cream	74
Mr Grey	80
Chocolate Lava S'mores	84
Tiramisu Jar	88
Ruby Raspberry & Rose Tart	92
Strawberries & Cream	96
Blackforest Jar	100
Tropical Panna Cotta Jar	106
Mille-Tuile	110
The Ultimate Praline Tart	114
Opera	120

PAGES

126 – 197

Nomtella	130
Bali Sunrise	134
Moss	140
An Apple a Day	146
Pear & Yuzu	150
Magic Mushrooms	154
Sitting in the Forest	162
Onyx	168
White Noise	174
Red Veil	180
Purple	186
Passion Berry Cheesecake Slice	194

LEVEL

2

KICKIN' IT UP A NOTCH

LEVEL

3

FOR THE SERIOUS COOKS

SPECIALTY INGREDIENTS	198
KITCHEN TOOLS	199
INDEX	200
ACKNOWLEDGEMENTS	204

INTRODUCTION

WE ALL LOVE FOOD, BUT WHEN YOU REALLY LOVE IT, YOU APPRECIATE AND UNDERSTAND THE CRAFTSMANSHIP AND THE POWER OF FOOD – WHETHER IT'S THROUGH THE PHILOSOPHY OF A FAMOUS CHEF OR YOUR GRANDMOTHER'S CONVICTION THAT HER GRANDKIDS NEED TO LEAVE HER HOUSE WITH A FULL BELLY.

Food plays a role much more important than just feeding the stomach – it's the universal love language of history and culture. And when it comes to desserts and baking, we can all relate to the way our brain reacts when we smell flour, eggs, sugar and sometimes chocolate wafting through the air as cakes or cookies bake in the oven. The sweet, warm aromas unlock a part of our brain that opens up our childhood memories, filling us with a sense of comfort or joy.

This was me when I was six or seven years old, somewhere a few hours' drive from Sydney. It was freezing and there was muddy snow. It's the only time I've seen snow ... grey, brown and slushie.

Many people have the clichéd memory of licking cake batter off a spatula, or baking chocolate cake with their grandmother. Growing up as an immigrant in Sydney, my childhood was a little bit different. Most of it was spent home alone looking after myself, and to be honest a lot of that time was spent snacking! My earliest dessert memory was when I was five years old, alone at home in the middle of summer and wanting a cheeky snack. I took a big scoop of vanilla ice cream out of the freezer and looked up in the kitchen at a high shelf that was filled with interesting bottles. Not knowing they were liqueurs and spirits, I remember thinking one of the dark bottles could be chocolate sauce. I hoisted my fearless young self up on the kitchen counter and climbed up to the shelf to grab the much-needed sauce for my ice cream. It ended up being a bottle of coffee liqueur. And let me tell you, it was delicious! I do remember thinking, *This chocolate tastes different*. But I loved it.

Here's eight-year-old me in my parents' restaurant, Bali Sunrise. After school, I'd sit and watch my parents work while I sipped on *cendol* (a coconut and pandan dessert drink) or a chocolate milkshake.

This was taken in Indonesia when I was three years old. Arnold is to my left and Ronald is to my right. I remember being upset that it was Ronald's birthday party and wishing it was mine.

Fast forward to the moment when I truly fell in love with food. It wasn't actually from tasting or smelling it; it was when I took a book from the shelf that held my mum's eclectic collection of cookbooks. Mum had books on the fundamentals of basic desserts to those of three-star Michelin chefs and restaurants, as well as some of the most iconic gods of modern fine dining, such as Gordon Ramsay, Ferran and Albert Adrià and Francisco Migoya. I found a very heavy book with a name that rolled off the tongue and ridiculous amounts of dishes that looked out of this world—it was *Alinea* by Grant Achatz. There were ingredients I'd never heard of and didn't know how to pronounce, but the book fascinated me. That was the moment when I realised that food is more than just nourishment—it can be an experience, as well as a platform for storytelling or a way to express yourself. Essentially, food is another form of art. *Alinea* amazed me with the colours, the recipes, the detail and the purpose of each dish. The recipes in the book were unachievable, especially for a fourteen-year-old kid, although I still challenged myself to try them. I was more fascinated by the biography, not just in *Alinea* but in many other cookbooks. I wanted to know how I could become a chef of such incredible calibre. That became one of the main drivers for me to work in food.

Throughout my high school years, my friends were obsessed with sports, sitcoms, surfing and skating. I was more obsessed with perfecting my chocolate tempering and crème caramels, and spherifying mangoes. Cooking became more than a hobby and fuelled a passion that saw me neglect my school work.

After I graduated from high school, my parents wouldn't let me pursue my dreams in food. Working in hospitality themselves, they knew the struggles of the industry and didn't want me to go through the same hardship. So they pushed me to pursue a degree (as is typical in many Asian families!), but I wasn't smart enough to get into the degrees that would make them proud. Naturally, I rebelled against my parents' wishes and tried to get a job in a high-end restaurant. Even though I asked to be paid a stupidly low wage (or not at all) and offered to do the dishes, I was rejected. I had no experience, but I was willing to learn.

In the end, defeated, I listened to my parents and pursued another field where I could still work with food, but also get myself into university (I actually had to do a diploma course before being admitted to a degree, but I failed twice). I studied nutrition but I dropped out in the first year because I was absolutely not diligent enough in studying. I was just obsessed with cooking. I'd watch Harvard University lectures on YouTube ... of chefs talking about food! I'd spend hours writing recipes and testing new dishes. It was a passion that would not die.

At KOI Dessert Bar, working the dinner menu service, plating in the hot section and desserts. On busy nights I would be running back and forth, making sure each dish was done right.

A little family portrait (Dad was working at the time): Arnold (left), Mum (middle), Ronald (top) and me (right). I don't know if we have an actual family photo!

During those years, Mum opened up a pastry kitchen in our home, selling to a cafe. I helped out by doing the washing, packing cakes and doing deliveries. I actually wasn't a huge fan of baking cakes – the classic sponge cake, blackforest or mud cake. I was more drawn to plated desserts where I could control and balance how much flavour was on the plate, and be more expressive in the presentation.

I also did volunteer work as a kitchen hand at a cafe in Bronte every Saturday for three months, helping the chefs prep during the day and cleaning up the kitchen at night, until one day I was asked to help with service. I really enjoyed the art of plating the food and the joy of watching beautiful food going out. But I couldn't afford to keep working for free. I remember I had just ten dollars in my pocket and I had overdrawn my bank account by fifty dollars. I had to use the ten dollars to put fuel in my car so I could make it to my university classes.

I ended up getting a paid job in another cafe for a few months. I would wake up at 5 a.m. every morning, chop a truckload of fruit, mash avocados, make bircher muesli and plate fruit salads for the breakfast and lunch shift, wrapping up by 4 or 5 p.m. But I had no joy – it was just whatever job I could get to put petrol in the car to be able to drive to university, which was 2 hours away from home.

Eventually, around the time I was given the opportunity of a lifetime to appear as a contestant on *MasterChef Australia 2015*, I dropped out of university. My girlfriend at the time, who I was constantly trying to impress with food, had pushed me to apply for the competition. Originally I wasn't keen, but I remember her saying, 'If you don't apply, I'm going to apply for you.' After leaving the competition in fourth place, my brothers, my mum and I joined forces to open KOI Dessert Bar and Monkey's Corner. And the rest is history. In the years since *MasterChef*, I've been grateful to be able to show the country and the world my love of food and cooking. Now I get to share it with you.

Most of my childhood and school years were spent teaching myself to create, cook and learn the basics and fundamentals of cooking. I've never trained under famous chefs for prolonged periods, or had the luxury of going to cooking school. But I was determined to create my own style of cooking and journey into this beautiful world of desserts. It goes to show that anyone can follow instructions and therefore anyone can cook. But I want you to take a step further and understand how to create by using these recipes as a foundation and guide. Remember that it's okay to fail, and trying again is what will make you a better cook. This is one of the reasons why I love what I do – there's always room for improvement and plenty to learn.

The cookbooks that I grew up with drew me into the path of loving food, stories and creativity. Cookbooks became a big part of the story of what inspired me to cook and I hope my book can be a part of your cooking journey, too. Seeing my first cookbook finally come to life has been a dream come true.

Some of the recipes curated in this book are from my childhood and some I'm still working on improving today. Whether you're a chef, a home cook or just starting out, I hope this book can teach you and guide you through successfully mastering a classic to building your very own artful creations at home. •

CHOOSE YOUR OWN FLAVOUR ADVENTURE

CHOCOLATE

These are some of the different flavour combinations that work well with chocolate. You could use as little as just one pairing or everything listed.

WHITE   MILK   DARK

WHITE	MILK	DARK
• Berries	• Caramel	• Coffee
• Pistachio	• Smoke	• Nuts
• Mint	• Nuts	• Caramel
• Vanilla	• Cheese	• Tart berries
• Citrus	• Honey	• Stone fruits
• Dried Apricot	• Spices	• Citrus
• Matcha	• Tonka bean	

WHITE CHOCOLATE

is sweet and plain on its own, which is what makes it such a great base and foundation to almost any flavour. I use a lot of my fruit-based crémeux and diplomat creams with white chocolate. You can also roast it and get the sugars and milk solids to caramelise, which completely changes the flavour profile and creates a new chocolate flavour.

Tonka bean

is a hard bean with vanilla, cinnamon, almond and clove flavours. Grate or steep the bean to release its unique flavour and aroma (it should never be eaten raw). Look for tonka beans in specialty hospitality stores or specialist spice retailers.

Throughout this book, you'll find that different components bounce and evolve from recipe to recipe, with minor ingredient changes, substitutions and additions. Once you get the hang of the basic recipes, try adding your own twist with different flavour combinations. Here are some of my favourites that will help you step up your dessert game.

P18 BROWNIE RECIPE

We've all got that family secret or our own twist to a good brownie recipe. Here's a basic guideline on how you can boost flavour, add texture and take your brownie game to the next level.

✚ NUTS

If you're a textural kind of person, add some crunch to your brownie with some nuts. (Personally, I like my brownie absolutely smooth and just plain-Jane fudgy.)

- Hazelnuts
- Peanuts
- Macadamias
- Pistachios

✚ SUGARS

Brownie recipes usually call for refined white sugar. Try substituting a dark sugar that will reduce the sweetness of your brownie and also add a depth of caramel-like flavour.

✚ LIQUEUR

Adding just a smidge of alcohol adds complexity to the brownie flavour – it's completely optional, but a fun addition. Add it to the batter at the last stage, just prior to baking.

- Dark spiced rum
- Pineapple rum
- Cointreau

✚ DRIED FRUITS

Dried fruits will add a touch of acidity and sweetness at the same time, as well as a little chewiness. It's best to add dried fruits as small chunks – dice and add them to the batter at the last stage, just prior to baking. Try using fruits that aren't rock hard, but have a higher sugar content and a gummy-like texture.

- Apricots
- Muscatels/raisins
- Cranberries

PALM SUGAR (jaggery)
is an unprocessed sugar that is derived from palm trees and has a smoky taste. It's best to use dark palm sugar, which is usually sold in round blocks, or gula melaka, which is another type of palm sugar.

MUSCOVADO SUGAR
is natural unrefined cane sugar that contains natural molasses.

DARK BROWN SUGAR
is sugar that contains a higher percentage of molasses. It has a deep and complex toffee and caramel flavour.

FRUIT CURDS = ACIDS

These consist of an acidic fruit juice combined with eggs, butter and sugar, which is then cooked until thickened to a custard-like consistency.

Using acidic fruit juice is crucial when it comes to making fruit curds, as fruit curds typically have a high sugar content. The acidic fruit juice will help reduce the sweetness and create a balanced fruit curd that isn't overly sweet, yet is still buttery, smooth and rich in texture.

TRY THESE ACIDS:
- Lemon • Lime
- Passionfruit
- Sea Buckthorn

Sea buckthorn is a rather tart, bright-orange berry, with a flavour resembling orange and mango. It's mostly grown and found in the northern hemisphere, but is often sold frozen in online stores.

ADD ACID TO THESE RECIPES:

P30 BUTTER CAKE

Create a **citrus** cream by folding a touch of whipped cream through **citrus** curd, then spread it on top of your butter cake and top it off with some freshly grated **citrus** zest. Amazing!

P54 RUM BA-BANANA

Pierce a hole in the middle of the cake and fill it with a dollop of **passionfruit** curd for an explosion of tropical flavour.

P58 ICE-CREAM SANDWICH

Add some grated ginger to the **lime** curd to add another layer of fragrant flavour.

CRÉMEUX

Crémeux, which means 'creamy' in French, is a dense, creamy pudding and it's freaking amazing in SO MANY WAYS! Versatile in flavour, texture, colour and application, crémeux is an essential component in the world of desserts.

BASIC CRÉMEUX

Adding whipped cream to the crémeux will transform the crémeux into an entirely new recipe called a **DIPLOMAT CREAM** which is a mousse-like cream.

A basic crémeux can either be made with just

CHOCOLATE AND ANGLAISE

e.g. Chocolate choux on page 40

CHOCOLATE/NUT PASTE/FRUIT AND CRÈME PÂTISSIÈRE

e.g. Moss on page 140

NUT PASTE

- Hazelnut
- Pistachio

FRUIT

- Raspberry
- Banana
- Passionfruit

CHOCOLATE

• Milk • Dark • White

If you're creating a crémeux using a nut paste, you'll need to add a small amount of bloomed gelatine and allow the crémeux to set overnight. The gelatine is important because nut pastes don't set completely – unlike chocolate, which sets at room temperature. However, you can use half nut paste and half chocolate – don't be afraid to experiment!

FOR EXAMPLE, FOR A BASIC CRÉMEUX YOU'LL NEED ...

2 eggs
10 g (¼ oz) white (granulated) sugar
150 ml (5 fl oz) full-cream milk
150 ml (5 fl oz) thickened (whipping) cream
100 g (3½ oz) nut paste
½ gelatine sheet (titanium grade)

LEVEL 1

TAKING
IT EASY

Perfect your
butter cake,
curd tart OR

Crème
caramel

Level 1

LET'S GET STARTED ON THE EASY STUFF, THE CROWD PLEASERS AND DESSERTS THAT YOU CAN DO WHETHER YOU'RE A BEGINNER OR AN EXPERT.

1 These are *quick, simple recipes* that most are familiar with, but with a little difference, whether that will be a substituted ingredient or a flavour pairing. Each recipe will *build your foundation* and allow you to open new doors to new flavours or techniques later down the track.

2 I feel like there are tons of basic recipes that are always so typical, obvious and repetitive, without much variety or anything new to offer. You'll notice how *easy* these recipes are and how doable they are at home, as well as how different they can be with little changes of ingredients, techniques or presentation. It'll give you that *extra edge*. Be daring in your kitchen!

3 So challenge yourself and don't forget that a great dish comes from *high-quality ingredients*. Try not to skimp on the building blocks, but if you really don't have the budget, that's okay — all of these dishes are still worth making.

BROWNIE

I think everyone should have a good brownie recipe in their repertoire. Brownies are pretty easy to make, but easy doesn't mean boring – there's nothing boring about an epic brownie! And let me point out that brownies don't have to be made with 'evil' processed white sugar. I've used muscovado sugar here because I love the flavour profile and it also reduces the sweetness. But it's not about health – after all, it's a brownie we're talking about!

You can have fun with this recipe and substitute ingredients – use palm sugar or brown sugar and try different blends of good-quality couverture chocolate, which is the key to an amazing brownie. Or replace the plain flour with coconut flour or another gluten-free alternative. Add some spices or even brown the butter before mixing it with the chocolate.

Oil spray, for greasing
270 g (9½ oz) 60% dark chocolate
250 g (9 oz) unsalted butter
240 g (8½ oz) muscovado sugar
2 pinches of salt
4 eggs
60 g (2¼ oz) plain (all-purpose) flour
80 g (2¾ oz) dark cocoa powder
1 teaspoon baking powder
50 g (1¾ oz) roasted hazelnuts,
    coarsely chopped
50 g (1¾ oz) slivered pistachios

Preheat the oven to 170°C (340°F). Line a 15 x 30 cm (6 x 12 inch) cake tin with baking paper and spray with oil.

Combine the chocolate, butter, muscovado sugar and salt in a heatproof bowl over a saucepan of simmering water and stir occasionally until melted. Remove from the heat and whisk in the eggs.

Sift the flour, cocoa and baking powder onto the chocolate mixture and fold until a batter is formed. Fold half of the hazelnuts and pistachios into the batter.

Spoon the batter into the tin and smooth the top. Scatter the remaining hazelnuts and pistachios over the batter in an even layer. Bake the brownie for 15–20 minutes. The centre will still be quite soft but will set once it cools (the brownie should be moist and fudgy – if it's too crumbly, it has been overcooked). Remove from the oven and set aside to cool to room temperature.

Remove the brownie from the tin and cut it into slices. Serve it to your loved ones ... or love yourself and dig in! The brownie is best when warmed a little in the microwave and served with a scoop of your favourite ice cream.

CRÈME CARAMEL

I remember making this dessert about ten years ago when I was sixteen or seventeen. It took me a while to get it right, but I had an obsession with perfecting a recipe, so here it is, one of my favourite dishes. I've added Baileys to this beautiful dessert because it actually helps to remove any eggy flavour, but you could also use a touch of rum. These are best enjoyed either chilled or warm.

CARAMEL

200 g (7 oz) caster (superfine) sugar

Put the sugar in a small, dry saucepan over medium heat. Cook the sugar, stirring occasionally as it melts and gently caramelises. Continue cooking until the caramel is a deep amber colour — it should be 160–166°C (320–331°F) on a sugar thermometer and at a smoking point without burning.

Remove the pan from the heat and carefully pour the caramel into six 180 ml (5½ fl oz) ramekins so that it reaches 1 cm (½ inch) up the sides. Set aside for the caramel to harden.

CUSTARD

500 ml (17 fl oz) full-cream milk
30 ml (1 fl oz) Baileys Irish Cream liqueur
Seeds of 1 vanilla bean
Rind of 1 lemon, peeled into strips
4 eggs
2 egg yolks
180 g (6 oz) caster (superfine) sugar

Preheat the oven to 150°C (300°F).

Combine the milk, Baileys, vanilla seeds and lemon rind in a saucepan and bring to a simmer.

Meanwhile, whisk the eggs, egg yolks and sugar in a heatproof bowl until fluffy. Slowly whisk in the hot milk mixture, being careful not to scald the eggs. (This is called 'tempering' the eggs.)

Strain the custard mixture into a jug and scoop out any foamy bits floating on top. (You can use a blowtorch to lightly 'kiss' the surface of the custard to remove any rogue bubbles.) Set aside to cool to room temperature.

Pour the custard mixture on top of the caramel in the ramekins, leaving a 1 cm (½ inch) gap at the top. Place the ramekins on a wire rack set in a roasting tin and pour in enough water to come halfway up the sides of the ramekins. Cover the roasting tin with foil.

Bake the crème caramels for 25–35 minutes or until they are set but wobble when given a slight shake. (If they're overcooked, the custard will be too firm and there will be a lot of air bubbles around the sides.) Remove the roasting tin from the oven and take the crème caramels out of the water bath. Set aside to cool a little, then either serve warm or place in the fridge to chill.

To serve, run a small knife around the edge of the custard to release it from the ramekin. Carefully flip it onto a serving plate and lift off the ramekin, allowing the caramel to spill over the side. Serve immediately.

BURNT HONEY BASQUE CHEESECAKE

I absolutely love basque cheesecake, although I had no idea what it was before the 2020 Basque cheesecake trend. In 2019, I went to Copenhagen to do a quick stagiaire at Alchemist 2.0. During my time there, I visited Hart Bageri and ordered a fat slice of cheesecake. Wow! It was insanely delicious, with an incredible, almost mousse-like texture. Little did I know, it was the Basque cheesecake but done differently. Since then, I've obsessed about this particular cheesecake that I'd never heard of, and I've failed many times in trying to recreate it. Finally, Chelia Dinata, who I helped start up ByCcino Cookies (in Bali), expanded her range, obsessed and experimented on countless Basque cheesecakes until she perfected it. So a very BIG thank you to her for sharing this wonderful recipe, which I've added my touches to.

CHEESECAKE

430 g (15¼ oz) cream cheese, softened
100 g (3½ oz) white (granulated) sugar
3 eggs
15 g (½ oz) plain (all-purpose) flour
270 ml (9½ fl oz) thickened (whipping) cream
15 ml (½ fl oz) lemon juice
Seeds of 1 vanilla bean

Preheat the oven to 200°C (400°F). Line an 18 cm (7 inch) spring-form cake tin with baking paper (I just get a big piece and punch it in to fit the tin).

Put the cream cheese and sugar in a mixer fitted with the paddle attachment and mix on medium speed for 5 minutes. Add the eggs, one at a time, and mix until well combined. Add the flour and mix for a further 3 minutes.

Slowly add the cream, lemon juice and vanilla seeds and mix until smooth and creamy, scraping down the side of the bowl to ensure there are no lumps.

Pour the cheesecake mixture into the tin. Bake for 25–27 minutes – the centre should still be wobbly. Allow the cheesecake to cool to room temperature, then place in the fridge.

BURNT HONEY GLAZE

150 g (5½ oz) honey
50 ml (1¾ fl oz) water

Put the honey in a small saucepan and cook over medium heat until the edges begin to caramelise and burn a little. Cook, stirring occasionally, until the honey has turned a deep amber, then slowly whisk in the water. (Be careful not to add the water too quickly as it will bubble and spit.) Bring the mixture to a simmer, then turn off the heat and set aside to cool to 35–40°C (95–104°F).

Evenly brush the cooled honey glaze over the dark surface of the cheesecake. Remove the cheesecake from the tin and serve chilled.

NOTE: If the honey glaze is rock hard once it's cooled, dilute it with some water. It should have the consistency of liquid glucose – if it's too firm to brush over the cheesecake, heat it in the microwave for 8–10 seconds to loosen.

CHOCOLATE MOUSSE

This mousse is next-level luxe. It's a little bit of a challenge because we're bringing in as much air as possible – into the yolks, the whites and the cream – to create a fluffy, velvety mouth feel. You can enjoy the mousse on its own or with fresh berries. I love serving it with homemade honeycomb or lemon jam (see page 29) ... or both, as I have done here. You could also fold in some crushed frozen raspberries along with the honeycomb and lemon jam. Perfection!

360 ml (12 fl oz) thickened
   (whipping) cream
3 eggs, separated
20 g (¾ oz) white (granulated) sugar
225 g (8 oz) 60% dark chocolate

Whip the cream until medium peaks form, then store it in the fridge until needed.

Combine the egg whites and half the sugar in a stand mixer and whisk until medium to stiff peaks form.

Meanwhile, melt the dark chocolate in a heatproof bowl in the microwave or over a saucepan of simmering water.

Combine the egg yolks and the remaining sugar in a heatproof bowl and whisk over a saucepan of simmering water until very fluffy to make a sabayon. Once the sabayon is glossy, slowly add the melted chocolate. (Don't worry if it firms up and looks a bit dry at this stage.) Remove the bowl from the heat.

Whisk in the meringue in three batches until the mixture is well combined, smooth and glossy. Using a rubber spatula, fold in the whipped cream in three batches until completely combined.

Pour the mousse into serving dishes or a container and put it in the fridge for about 45 minutes to set.

NOTE: You can flavour the melted chocolate with a pistachio paste, hazelnut paste or praline paste. Substitute 20–30% of the chocolate weight with the flavouring of your choice. You can also use milk chocolate or white chocolate. →

HONEYCOMB

160 g (5½ oz) caster (superfine) sugar
60 g (2¼ oz) liquid glucose
25 g (1 oz) honey
7.5 g (¼ oz) bicarbonate of soda
(baking soda)

Line a 15 x 30 x 8 cm (6 x 12 x 3¼ inch) cake tin with baking paper.

Combine the sugar, glucose and honey in a saucepan. Cook over medium heat until the mixture reaches 156°C (313°F) on a sugar thermometer. Remove the pan from the heat and quickly but carefully whisk in the bicarbonate of soda as the mixture will bubble up very quickly. Immediately pour the mixture into the tin. Allow the honeycomb to cool down and set for about 30 minutes.

Break the honeycomb into chunks and serve it on top of the mousse. You can also fold the honeycomb through the mousse. Store any left-over honeycomb in an airtight container for up to a week.

LEMON JAM

1 large lemon
50 g (1¾ oz) white (granulated) sugar
50 ml (1¾ fl oz) water

Cut off the top and bottom of the lemon. Using a sharp peeler, carefully remove the peel in strips, then use a small knife to remove as much of the pith as possible. Slice the lemon zest strips as thinly as possible, then finely chop them and place them in a saucepan.

Segment the lemon and add the segments to the pan with the chopped zest. Squeeze the juice from the remaining lemon flesh and add it to the pan along with the sugar.

Cook the lemon mixture over medium heat for 30–35 minutes or until golden and caramelised – there should be little or no liquid left. Add the water to deglaze the pan and stir with a rubber spatula to remove anything that has stuck to the pan. Remove from the heat and set aside to cool.

Place a little layer of the lemon jam in serving cups and top it with the mousse so there's a little sour surprise. Store the left-over jam in an airtight container in the fridge for up to 2 months.

NOTE: This lemon jam is super concentrated. It has a nice bitterness from the caramelisation, as well as a touch of sweetness. It pairs perfectly with the rich chocolate mousse, but you won't need much.

THE BEST BASIC BUTTER CAKE

These are the easiest cakes I've ever made. They're also mega tasty and so versatile, and you can flavour them in many ways. Try adding a teaspoon of ground cinnamon along with the flour, or top the batter with just one or various fruits, which will also form a garnish. Make fig butter cakes by arranging sliced figs on top of the batter, or fold some crushed frozen raspberries through the batter for raspberry butter cakes – get creative!

I recommend enjoying these butter cakes while they're still slightly warm, with a hot cup of tea.

250 g (9 oz) unsalted butter, softened
210 g (7½ oz) caster (superfine) sugar
200 g (7 oz) self-raising flour
2 pinches of fine salt
3 eggs
185 ml (6 fl oz) full-cream milk
Grated zest and juice of ½ lemon
20 g (¾ oz) honey, plus 50 g (1¾ oz)
    for brushing
20 ml (¾ fl oz) extra virgin olive oil
Fruit of your choice (see Notes)

Preheat the oven to 180°C (350°F). Line five 10 cm (4 inch) spring-form cake tins with baking paper.

Put the butter and sugar in an electric mixer fitted with the whisk attachment. Whisk on medium–high speed until fluffy, about 5–8 minutes. Meanwhile, sift the flour and salt together.

Once the butter mixture is fluffy, add the eggs, one at a time, and whisk until combined. Add the milk, lemon zest, lemon juice, honey and olive oil and whisk until completely incorporated. Add the sifted flour and slowly whisk until a batter is formed.

Spoon 190 g (6¾ oz) of the batter into each cake tin. Arrange thin slices or pieces of fruit on top.

Bake the cakes for 35–40 minutes or until a skewer inserted into the centre of each one comes out clean.

Warm the honey in the microwave for 10–20 seconds to loosen it. Drizzle each hot cake with some of the honey and use a pastry brush to brush it over the top of the cake. Allow the cakes to cool a little before removing them from the tins and brushing them with more honey.

NOTES: Try using thinly sliced or chopped apples, oranges, figs or berries on top of the cakes. Ensure the fruit isn't too bulky or it will sink into the batter. You can also cook the batter in one large cake tin. Increase the cooking time by about 15–30 minutes, depending on the size of the tin.

MATCHA & YUZU GANACHE TART

I love matcha desserts, especially this simple ganache tart. The cold fudge bite as your teeth sink into the ganache and the crumbly pastry ... it's awesome. This tart is the ultimate in flavour, with bitter, sweet, sour and salty notes in every mouthful.

MATCHA TART SHELL

375 g (13 oz) plain (all-purpose) flour, plus extra for dusting

80 g (2¾ oz) white (granulated) sugar

200 g (7 oz) chilled unsalted butter, cubed

20 g (¾ oz) matcha powder (see Notes)

1 egg

1 egg yolk

100 g (3½ oz) white chocolate

Preheat the oven to 170°C (340°F). Place a 17 x 2 cm (6½ x ¾ inch) perforated tart ring on a baking tray lined with baking paper.

Combine the flour, sugar, butter and matcha powder in a mixer fitted with the paddle attachment. Mix until a sandy texture is formed. Slowly add the egg and the egg yolk and mix until a dough is formed. Wrap the dough in plastic wrap and refrigerate for at least 30 minutes.

Roll out the dough on a lightly floured surface to a thickness of 2 mm (1⁄16 inch). Drape the dough over the tart ring and tuck in the edges, cutting off the excess. Prick the centre with a skewer a few times. Line the tart shell with baking paper and fill with baking beads or uncooked rice. Blind bake the shell for 15 minutes. Remove the paper and beads or rice and bake for a further 15 minutes or until golden. Set aside to cool.

Melt the white chocolate in a heatproof bowl in the microwave or over a saucepan of simmering water. Coat the inside of the tart shell with the melted chocolate and allow it to set.

MATCHA & YUZU GANACHE

200 ml (7 fl oz) single (pure) cream

30 g (1 oz) liquid glucose

50 ml (1¾ fl oz) yuzu juice (see Notes)

250 g (9 oz) white chocolate

25 g (1 oz) matcha powder (see Notes), plus extra for dusting

50 g (1¾ oz) unsalted butter

Combine the cream, liquid glucose and yuzu juice in a saucepan and stir over medium heat until simmering.

Put the white chocolate and matcha powder in a heatproof jug. Pour in the hot cream mixture and use an immersion blender to blend in the chocolate. Add the butter and blend until glossy and smooth. Cool the ganache to room temperature.

Pour the cooled ganache into the chocolate-coated tart shell. Place the tart in the fridge for 2–3 hours or until set.

Just before serving, dust the tart with matcha powder.

NOTES: You don't need an expensive, A-grade matcha powder for this recipe – those are for drinking. Yuzu juice is sold in Asian grocers but it can be difficult to source. You can omit it or replace it with lime or calamansi juice, although these won't add the same fragrance as the yuzu.

CITRUS MERINGUE TART

START THIS RECIPE
A DAY AHEAD

A citrus meringue tart is usually topped with an Italian meringue. I wanted to make my tart less sweet and also be a little bit creative by not only flavouring the tart shell, but also changing the way it's filled and garnished. The meringue is cooked as a disc and then broken into pieces so the gorgeous filling shows through.

CITRUS CURD

100 ml (3½ fl oz) lemon juice
65 g (2¼ oz) unsalted butter
Grated zest of 1 orange
4 eggs
100 g (3½ oz) caster (superfine)
    sugar

Combine the lemon juice, butter and orange zest in a saucepan. Cook over medium heat until simmering. Meanwhile, whisk the eggs and sugar in a heatproof bowl until fluffy.

Whisk the hot lemon mixture into the egg mixture. Place the bowl over a saucepan of simmering water. Cook, stirring once every couple of minutes, until the mixture has thickened.

Transfer the hot citrus curd mixture to a jug and blend with an immersion blender until smooth. Pass the curd through a fine sieve and store it in a container in the fridge overnight.

FRENCH EARL GREY TART SHELL

375 g (13 oz) plain (all-purpose) flour,
    plus extra for dusting
80 g (2¾ oz) white (granulated)
    sugar
200 g (7 oz) chilled unsalted butter,
    cubed
6 g (⅛ oz) French Earl Grey tea,
    ground to a fine powder
1 egg
1 egg yolk
50 g (1¾ oz) white chocolate

Preheat the oven to 170°C (340°F). Place two 17 x 2 cm (6½ x ¾ inch) perforated tart rings on a baking tray lined with baking paper.

Combine the flour, sugar, butter and ground tea in a mixer fitted with the paddle attachment. Mix until a sandy texture is formed. Slowly add the egg and egg yolk and mix until a dough is formed. Wrap the dough in plastic wrap and refrigerate for at least 30 minutes.

Divide the chilled dough in half. Roll out one portion of the dough on a lightly floured surface to a thickness of 3–5 mm (⅛–¼ inch). Drape the dough over one of the tart rings and tuck in the edges, cutting off the excess. Repeat with the remaining dough. Prick the centre of each tart shell with a skewer a few times. Line the shells with baking paper and fill with baking beads or uncooked rice. Blind bake the shells for 15 minutes. Remove the paper and beads or rice and bake for a further 15 minutes or until golden. Set aside to cool.

Melt the white chocolate in a heatproof bowl in the microwave or over a saucepan of simmering water. Coat the inside of each tart shell with the melted chocolate and allow it to set. Once set, remove the tart shells from the tart rings. →

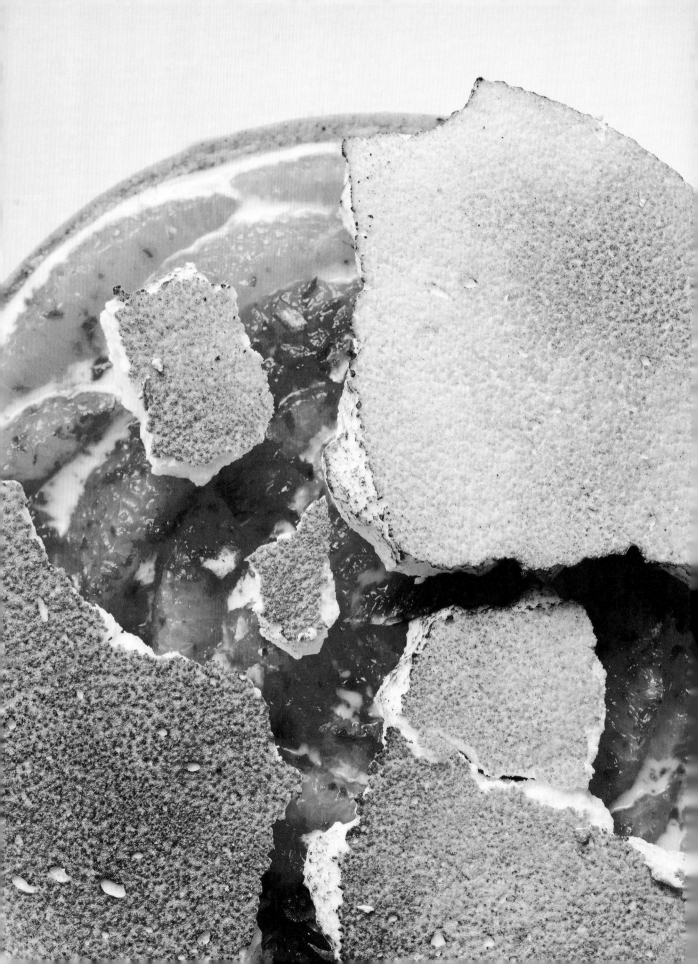

MERINGUE DISC

Oil spray, for greasing
85 g (3 oz) egg whites
170 g (5¾ oz) caster (superfine) sugar

Wash and dry the tart rings that were used to cook the tart shells. Lightly spray the inside of the rings with oil and place them on a silicone baking mat.

Put the egg whites and sugar in a mixer fitted with the whisk attachment and whisk until stiff peaks form.

Pipe the meringue into each tart ring in a circular motion until it reaches just below the top of the ring. Remove the tart rings. Place the meringue discs in a dehydrator at 70°C (150°F) for 2–3 hours or until crisp. Leave to cool completely, then store the meringue discs in an airtight container.

NOTE: If you don't have a dehydrator, you can cook the meringue discs in a 70°C (150°F) oven instead.

ASSEMBLY

4 navel oranges, segmented
20 g (¾ oz) freeze-dried blood
    orange

Arrange the orange segments over the base of the tart shells. Crumble the freeze-dried blood orange over the top of the orange segments.

Transfer the citrus curd to a piping bag and pipe it on top of the citrus segments, leaving a small gap at the top of the tart shells.

Remove the meringue discs from the dehydrator. Using a microplane, shave the discs if needed to create perfect circles that are the same size as the tarts. Place the meringue discs on a chopping board and, using the back of a spoon, lightly crack the centre of each disc. Arrange the broken pieces of meringue on top of the citrus curd. Use a blowtorch to lightly brown the meringue.

NOTE: Replace the navel oranges with blood oranges when they're in season and omit the freeze-dried blood orange. You can also use other citrus fruit, such as grapefruit or pomelo.

CHOCOLATE CHOUX

START THIS RECIPE
A DAY AHEAD

Ahh, the choux pastry. It can be daunting trying to get the perfect rise and crunch, but it's all about timing, instinct and practice. Choux is your passport to profiteroles, eclairs and the croquembouche. You'll want to sink your teeth into these buns because they're so irresistibly sexy! Plus, they have a lovely craquelin topping that not only looks good, it adds more crunch.

The chocolate crémeux is best made a day ahead so that it can set to a beautiful smooth and creamy texture.

CHOCOLATE CRÉMEUX

150 ml (5 fl oz) full-cream milk
150 ml (5 fl oz) single (pure) cream
2 eggs
10 g (¼ oz) caster (superfine) sugar
150 g (5½ oz) milk chocolate
100 g (3½ oz) dark chocolate

Combine the milk and cream in a saucepan and bring to the boil.

Meanwhile, whisk the eggs and sugar in a heatproof bowl until fluffy. Whisk in the hot milk mixture, then pour the mixture back into the pan and cook until it reaches 83°C (181°F) on a sugar thermometer. Remove from the heat.

Add the chocolate and whisk until melted and smooth. Strain the crémeux into a container and refrigerate overnight.

NOTE: You can also flavour the chocolate crémeux with other ingredients, such as pistachio paste or even peanut butter. Substitute 20–30% of the total weight of the chocolate with the flavouring of your choice.

CHOCOLATE CRAQUELIN

50 g (1¾ oz) butter
50 g (1¾ oz) white (granulated) sugar
50 g (1¾ oz) almond meal
25 g (1 oz) plain (all-purpose) flour
5 g (⅛ oz) dark cocoa powder

Put the butter and sugar in a mixer fitted with the paddle attachment and mix until the butter is softened. Add the almond meal, flour and cocoa and mix until a dough is formed.

Roll out the dough between two sheets of baking paper until it is 1 mm (about 1/16 inch) thick. Transfer the paper and dough to a tray and place in the freezer until the dough is solid.

Remove the tray from the freezer and use a 5 cm (2 inch) round cutter to cut eight circles from the dough, re-rolling the excess to cut out more circles. Return the craquelin circles to the freezer until needed.

NOTE: You can also make a plain craquelin by omitting the cocoa powder, or replace the cocoa with 7.5 g (¼ oz) of matcha powder to make a matcha-flavoured craquelin. ➜

CHOUX BUNS

130 ml (4 fl oz) water
50 g (1¾ oz) unsalted butter
Pinch of salt
75 g (2½ oz) plain (all-purpose) flour
2 eggs

Preheat the oven to 180°C (350°F). Line a large baking tray with a silicone mat or baking paper.

Combine the water, butter and salt in a saucepan. Bring to the boil over medium heat, then add the flour and cook, stirring with a spatula, for 2–3 minutes or until the batter is coming off the side of the pan.

Transfer the hot roux to a mixer fitted with the paddle attachment. Mix the dough on medium–high speed until there is no more steam. Slowly add the eggs, one at a time, and mix until completely combined. The dough should be smooth and viscous but not runny.

Transfer the dough to a piping bag fitted with a 2.5 cm (1 inch) round nozzle. Pipe the dough onto a baking tray in 15 g (½ oz) balls, leaving a 5 cm (2 inch) gap between each to allow for spreading. Place a circle of frozen craquelin dough on top of each dough ball and bake for 45–50 minutes or until the choux is golden and the craquelin has darkened. Set the buns aside to cool to room temperature on the tray.

ASSEMBLY

Dark cocoa powder, for dusting

Poke a hole in the base of each bun with a chopstick or small knife.

Transfer the chocolate crémeux to a piping bag. Pipe the crémeux into the buns, filling them completely.

Lightly dust the buns with cocoa powder.

VARIATIONS: You can also cut the buns in half and use a star nozzle to pipe the crémeux onto the bases before replacing the tops. Omit the craquelin topping if you prefer, and simply fill the choux buns with whipped cream.

To make eclairs, pipe the choux dough into 15 cm (6 inch) lengths before baking, and top each with a 3 x 15 cm (1¼ x 6 inch) strip of the craquelin dough. Poke three holes in the base of each eclair before filling them with the chocolate crémeux. Alternatively, you can cut the eclairs in half lengthways and use a star nozzle to pipe a line of crémeux down the centre before replacing the tops.

To make Paris-Brest, replace the dark chocolate in the chocolate crémeux with hazelnut paste to make a hazelnut crémeux. Use a 2 cm (¾ inch) star nozzle to pipe the choux dough into 8 cm (3¼ inch) rings, and top each with a ring cut from the craquelin dough before baking. Once cooled, cut the Paris-Brest in half horizontally and use the star nozzle to pipe the hazelnut crémeux onto each base, then replace the tops. Pipe small dollops of hazelnut crémeux on each Paris-Brest and top each dollop with a roasted hazelnut half. Lightly dust with dark cocoa powder and icing (confectioners') sugar.

INDIVIDUAL PAVLOVAS

Whether this classic belongs to the Aussies or the Kiwis, it doesn't really matter. It's a timeless dessert with endless possibilities. The pavlova itself is the perfect vessel for so many different flavours and toppings throughout all of the seasons. Here are my favourite versions – Spiced apple pavlovas (top left, see page 48), Boozy berry pavlovas (middle, see page 52) and Cherry & coconut pavlovas (bottom left, see page 47) ... there's something for every season and palate.

150 g (5½ oz) egg whites *(see Note)*
300 g (10½ oz) caster (superfine) sugar
10 g (¼ oz) cornflour (cornstarch)

Preheat the oven to 100°C (200°F). Line a baking tray with baking paper.

Combine the egg whites and sugar in a mixer fitted with the whisk attachment. Whisk until medium peaks form. Sift the cornflour onto the mixture and whisk at full speed until stiff peaks form.

Transfer the meringue to a piping bag fitted with a 3 cm (1¼ inch) round nozzle. Carefully pipe four large dollops of meringue onto the tray, about 7.5 cm (3 inches) wide and 5 cm (2 inches) high. (Alternatively, spoon the meringue onto the tray and shape it to the desired size.)

Bake the pavlovas for 50 minutes or until slightly beige in colour. Remove the tray from the oven and allow the pavlovas to cool completely. Once cooled, gently poke a hole in the top of each one – the pavlovas should be hollow with a marshmallowy base.

NOTE: You'll need about 4 egg whites for this recipe, depending on the size of the eggs.

CHERRY & COCONUT PAVLOVAS

START THIS RECIPE
A DAY AHEAD

I've matched this iconic flavour pairing with the iconic Aussie pavlova. Australian cherries with a smidge of coconut and chocolate … this is an epic summer dessert. The cherry reduction is an optional extra for those willing to go the extra mile.

DARK CHOCOLATE CRÉMEUX

150 ml (5 fl oz) full-cream milk
150 ml (5 fl oz) single (pure) cream
2 eggs
10 g (¼ oz) caster (superfine) sugar
250 g (9 oz) 60–70% dark chocolate

Combine the milk and cream in a saucepan and bring to the boil.

Meanwhile, whisk the eggs and sugar in a heatproof bowl until fluffy. Whisk in the hot milk mixture, then pour the mixture back into the pan and cook until it reaches 83°C (181°F) on a sugar thermometer. Remove the pan from the heat.

Add the chocolate and whisk until melted and smooth. Strain the crémeux into a container and refrigerate overnight.

COCONUT PAVLOVAS

1 quantity pavlova mixture (page 44)
50 g (1¾ oz) desiccated coconut

Prepare four individual pavlovas following the method on page 44, lightly coating the tops of the meringues with coconut before baking.

CHERRY COMPOTE

300 g (10½ oz) cherries, pitted
40 g (1½ oz) caster (superfine) sugar
150 ml (5 fl oz) water
2 pinches of citric acid

Combine the cherries, sugar, water and citric acid in a saucepan. Cook over medium heat until the cherries have broken down and the mixture has a jam-like consistency.

Transfer the compote to a container and refrigerate until needed.

CHERRY REDUCTION

300 g (10½ oz) cherries, pitted
35 g (1¼ oz) liquid glucose
Pinch of citric acid, or to taste

Juice the cherries in a cold-press juicer. Strain the juice into a small saucepan, discarding the pulp. Add the glucose and citric acid to the cherry juice and cook over low heat until the liquid has reduced to a viscous sauce. Set aside to cool to room temperature.

ASSEMBLY

10 cherries, pitted and halved
Desiccated coconut, for sprinkling

Transfer the chocolate crémeux to a piping bag and pipe it into the pavlovas until they are two-thirds full. Spoon the cherry compote on top. Garnish with the cherry halves, drizzle with cherry reduction and sprinkle with coconut. Serve immediately.

SPICED APPLE PAVLOVAS

START THIS RECIPE
A DAY AHEAD

This recipe is a different take on a pavlova and it's lovely for autumn or even winter. It uses every part of the apple (except the core, of course). The skin is amazing when it's caramelised and the juice is cooked down to create a sweet, sour, concentrated apple caramel sauce. It's a creative way to use all of the apple and reduce waste. It does involve a bit of extra effort, but it's well worth it, in my opinion. If you're looking for a quick recipe, just make the spiced apple filling and leave out the caramelised apple skin and apple caramel.

SALTED VANILLA WHIPPED GANACHE

½ gelatine sheet (titanium grade)
385 ml (13 fl oz) thickened (whipping) cream
5 g (⅛ oz) salt
Seeds of 1 vanilla bean
100 g (3 ½ oz) white chocolate

Soak the gelatine in cold water to soften.

Pour 165 ml (5½ fl oz) of the cream into a saucepan, add the salt and vanilla seeds and bring to a simmer over medium heat.

Put the white chocolate in a heatproof bowl, pour in the hot cream and stir until melted. Squeeze the excess water from the softened gelatine, add it to the cream mixture and stir until dissolved and well combined. Pass the mixture through a fine sieve, then allow it to cool to room temperature.

Stir in the remaining 220 ml (7½ fl oz) of cream. Pour the ganache into an airtight container and refrigerate overnight.

Transfer the ganache to a mixer fitted with the whisk attachment. Whisk until the mixture is very smooth and has formed medium peaks. Transfer to a piping bag and place in the fridge until needed.

CINNAMON PAVLOVAS

1 quantity pavlova mixture (page 44)
6 g (⅛ oz) ground cinnamon

Prepare four individual pavlovas following the method on page 44, sifting the cinnamon into the meringue mixture along with the cornflour.

SPICED APPLE MIX

500 g (1 lb 2 oz) green apples
50 g (1¾ oz) unsalted butter
1 cinnamon stick or cassia bark
2 star anise
4 cloves
Juice of ½ lemon
1 lemon zest strip
100 g (3½ oz) soft brown sugar

Peel and core the apples, reserving the skin to make the caramelised apple skin (see page 51). Roughly dice the flesh into 1 cm (½ inch) cubes. Juice any apple off-cuts through a cold-press juicer and set aside for the apple caramel (see page 51).

Melt the butter in a saucepan over medium heat. Add the whole spices and cook for 2–3 minutes or until fragrant. Add the diced apple, lemon juice and lemon zest and cook, stirring, for 5 minutes. Stir in the brown sugar and cook for 10–15 minutes or until the apple just begins to turn translucent. Don't overcook the apple or it will become mushy and lose its structure. Remove the pan from the heat and transfer the mixture to an airtight container to cool. →

CARAMELISED APPLE SKIN

Peeled apple skins (*see spiced apple mix, page 48*)
Caster (superfine) sugar, for rolling

Preheat the oven to 160°C (320°F). Line a baking tray with baking paper. Roll the apple skins in the sugar, then spread them out on the baking tray.

Bake for 10–15 minutes or until the apple skins turn golden brown. Set aside to cool. The apple skins should become crisp.

APPLE CARAMEL

300 ml (10½ fl oz) fresh apple juice (*see Note*)
50 ml (1¾ fl oz) water

Pour the apple juice into a saucepan and cook over low heat, reducing the juice until it becomes viscous. Increase the heat and cook until the edges begin to brown, stirring with a spatula to ensure it doesn't burn.

Slowly whisk in the water to help loosen the sugars so that the caramel forms a glaze. Be careful not to add the water too quickly as it will boil and spit.

NOTE: Use the juice made from the left-over apple in the spiced apple mix. Top it up with some more freshly squeezed apple juice or bottled apple juice, if needed.

ASSEMBLY

Spoon the salted vanilla whipped ganache into the hollow cinnamon pavlovas until they are half full, then add the spiced apple mix.

Garnish the pavlovas with shards of the caramelised apple skin and drizzle the apple caramel over the top.

BOOZY BERRY PAVLOVAS

Perfect for spring or summer, this is basically a classic pavlova ... but even better! We're boozin' it up and bringing in some more floral notes to really round out the fragrant berries. These little touches are a beautiful upgrade of the classic.

MACERATED BERRIES

5 large mint leaves
100 g (3½ oz) blueberries
100 g (3½ oz) strawberries, quartered
50 ml (1¾ fl oz) bourbon or whisky
70 g (2½ oz) soft brown sugar
Grated zest and juice of ½ lime

Roll the mint leaves and chiffonade — that's a fancy way of saying finely chop the mint leaves. You want to chop them, not bruise them, so make sure your knife is really sharp.

Combine the berries, bourbon or whisky, brown sugar, lime zest, lime juice and mint in a bowl and lightly toss together. Refrigerate the mixture for 30–45 minutes to allow the berries to release their juices.

ELDERFLOWER CHANTILLY

300 ml (10½ fl oz) thickened (whipping) cream
45 g (1½ oz) caster (superfine) sugar
30 ml (1 fl oz) elderflower syrup

Combine the cream, sugar and elderflower syrup in a mixer fitted with the whisk attachment. Whisk until stiff peaks form.

Transfer the elderflower chantilly to a piping bag (or store it in an airtight container in the fridge if you're not using it straight away).

ASSEMBLY

4 individual pavlovas (page 44)
1 lime

Fill the pavlovas with the elderflower chantilly and then spoon the macerated berries on top, letting them overflow, with the juices dripping down the sides.

Use a microplane to grate lime zest over the pavlovas. Serve immediately.

RUM BA-BANANA & PINEAPPLE

We are switchin' things up here! Usually rum baba is just a plain yeast cake soaked in rum and served with pastry cream. Where's the flavour in the cake – yeast and sugar? I object to plain cake! Here I've added banana – sure, it's not traditional, but so what? We're improving it, so let's look at the flavours we're building. Dark rum has a flavour profile that goes well with spices. And what else goes well with spices? Banana, of course! Then it's all tied together with some acidity and freshness – charred pineapple and lime zest, to really give it a lift.

BA-BANANA CAKES

Butter, for greasing
70 ml (2¼ fl oz) full-cream milk
30 ml (1 fl oz) thickened (whipping) cream
2 g (¹⁄₁₆ oz) dry yeast
150 g (5½ oz) very ripe banana, mashed (see Notes)
150 g (5½ oz) dark brown sugar (see Notes)
Seeds of 1 vanilla bean
2 eggs
100 g (3½ oz) unsalted butter, melted
200 g (7 oz) plain (all-purpose) flour
Pinch of salt

Lightly grease six 150 ml (5 fl oz) dariole moulds with butter.

Pour the milk and cream into a mug and heat it in the microwave until it reaches 30–35°C (86–95°F) on a sugar thermometer. Stir in the yeast and set aside.

Meanwhile, lightly combine the banana, brown sugar and vanilla seeds in a mixer fitted with the paddle attachment. Mix in the eggs, one at a time, then pour in the melted butter and continue mixing. Fold in the flour. Add the milk mixture and salt and mix until well combined.

Transfer the dough to the dariole moulds, filling them two-thirds full. Set aside in a warm place for 25–30 minutes or until the dough reaches the tops of the moulds. Meanwhile, preheat the oven to 170°C (340°F).

Bake the cakes for 15–20 minutes or until the tops are golden. Allow the cakes to cool in the moulds, then turn them out onto a wire rack to cool completely.

NOTES: Use super-ripe bananas that are really mushy and brown, and mash them to a paste. You can use regular brown sugar instead of dark brown sugar. The cakes can be quite dense if they are not proved properly, so be sure not to rush it.

RUM SYRUP

150 ml (5 fl oz) dark rum (I recommend Captain Morgan rum or Plantation Pineapple rum)
200 ml (7 fl oz) water
100 g (3½ oz) caster (superfine) sugar

Combine the rum, water and sugar in a saucepan. Bring to the boil over medium–high heat and cook until the mixture has reduced to a syrup, about 20 minutes. Remove from the heat and set aside until needed. →

BARBECUED PINEAPPLE

½ pineapple
150 g (5½ oz) caster (superfine) sugar
2 star anise
1 cinnamon stick
6 saffron threads

Remove the skin and core of the pineapple. Cut the pineapple into thick batons and place in a deep bowl. Add the sugar and spices and gently toss to coat the pineapple. Set aside to marinate for 30 minutes.

Heat a barbecue or chargrill pan to high. Cook the marinated pineapple until evenly charred on all sides.

Once the pineapple is cool enough to handle, cut it into small cubes. Set aside to cool completely.

NOTE: This would be perfect to cook over charcoal, adding extra smokiness to the dish, or you can cheat and use a blowtorch.

CRÈME FRAÎCHE & LIME CHANTILLY

200 ml (7 fl oz) thickened
    (whipping) cream
100 g (3½ oz) crème fraîche
30 g (1 oz) icing (confectioners') sugar
Grated zest and juice of ½ lime

Whisk the cream, crème fraîche and sugar together. Add the lime zest and lime juice and whip until stiff peaks form. Transfer the chantilly to a container and refrigerate until serving.

ASSEMBLY

Grated lime zest, to garnish

Warm the ba-banana cakes in the oven for 5–8 minutes or microwave for 30–60 seconds.

Meanwhile, bring the rum syrup to a simmer.

Place the warm cakes on individual plates and soak them with rum syrup. Add a generous dollop of the crème fraîche and lime chantilly and a spoonful of the barbecued pineapple. Drizzle more of the rum syrup over the cakes and garnish with grated lime zest.

ORANGE BLOSSOM ICE-CREAM SANDWICH WITH LIME CURD

START THIS RECIPE
A DAY AHEAD

Welcome to the textural experience of an epic ice-cream sandwich that will really tingle your tastebuds. We're using everything that citrus can offer, from the floral notes of orange blossom water in the orange blossom parfait to the zing of lime juice and the fragrance of lime zest in the lime curd. And what better way to sandwich it all together than with a crunchy almond sablé?

ORANGE BLOSSOM & VANILLA PARFAIT

½ gelatine sheet (titanium grade)
3 egg yolks
40 g (1½ oz) caster (superfine) sugar
Seeds of 1 vanilla bean
100 g (3½ oz) white chocolate
220 ml (7½ fl oz) thickened (whipping) cream
20 ml (½ fl oz) orange blossom water

Line a 15 x 30 cm (6 x 12 inch) cake tin with baking paper.

Soak the gelatine in cold water to soften.

Combine the egg yolks, sugar and vanilla seeds in a heatproof bowl and whisk over a saucepan of simmering water until fluffy to make a sabayon. Add the white chocolate and whisk until melted. Squeeze the excess water from the softened gelatine, add it to the sabayon and stir until dissolved and well combined.

Whip the cream until medium peaks form, then fold the cream into the sabayon, followed by the orange blossom water.

Pour the parfait mixture into the cake tin and freeze overnight.

Line a tray with baking paper. Remove the frozen parfait from the tin and cut it into four or five even rectangles. Place the parfait slices on the tray and return them to the freezer to firm up.

Using a 6 cm (2½ inch) round cutter, cut four or five circles out of the parfait. Working quickly, use a 2 cm (¾ inch) round cutter to remove the centre of each parfait circle. Return the parfait rings to the freezer until ready to serve.

NOTES: Add the finely grated zest of 1 orange and/or some finely chopped orange segments to the parfait mixture for extra texture. You can serve the parfait in slices if you don't want to make ice-cream sandwiches. →

LIME CURD

100 ml (3½ fl oz) lime juice
Finely grated zest of 1 lime
65 g (2¼ oz) unsalted butter
4 eggs
100 g (3½ oz) caster (superfine)
   sugar

Combine the lime juice, lime zest and butter in a saucepan. Cook over medium heat until simmering. Meanwhile, whisk the eggs and sugar in a heatproof bowl until fluffy.

Whisk the hot lime and butter mixture into the egg mixture. Place the bowl over a saucepan of simmering water. Cook, stirring once every couple of minutes, until the mixture has thickened.

Transfer the hot lime curd to a jug and blend with an immersion blender until smooth. Pass the lime curd through a fine sieve and store it in a container in the fridge overnight.

ALMOND SABLÉ

105 g (3½ oz) unsalted butter
80 g (2¾ oz) caster (superfine) sugar
80 g (2¾ oz) almond meal
200 g (7 oz) plain (all-purpose) flour
2 pinches of salt
1 egg

Preheat the oven to 170°C (340°F).

Combine the butter, sugar, almond meal, flour and salt in a mixer fitted with the paddle attachment. Mix on medium speed until a sandy texture is formed, then add the egg and mix until a dough is formed.

Roll out the dough between two sheets of baking paper until it is 1–2 mm (about ¹⁄₁₆ inch) thick. Transfer the paper and dough to a baking tray, then remove the top sheet of baking paper.

Bake the sablé for 15–17 minutes or until golden brown. Remove from the oven and immediately cut out eight or ten rounds using a 6 cm (2½ inch) round cutter. Allow the sablé to cool before separating the rounds from the excess sablé. Store the sablé rounds in an airtight container.

NOTE: Be sure to cut the sablé rounds as soon as the sablé comes out of the oven, otherwise it won't be possible to cut. You can reserve the excess sablé to make a cheesecake base. It can be frozen for 3–4 months.

ASSEMBLY

Transfer the chilled lime curd to a piping bag.

Place each parfait ring on an almond sablé round and fill the centre with the lime curd. Place another almond sablé round on top of each parfait ring and serve immediately or place in the freezer until serving.

NOTE: Use the excess lime curd in the Citrus meringue tart (page 36) or spoon it into an empty tart shell to make a simple lime curd tart. The lime curd will keep in the fridge for up to 2–3 months.

VIN & GRAPES

This is a thoughtful summer dessert that uses grapes and wine together—a journey from fruit to wine. It's perfect for dinner parties, with three simple components that will go a long way when done well. It does take a bit of time and effort, but if you're out to impress, this one is a winner.

CHARDONNAY MOUSSE

200 ml (7 fl oz) chardonnay
1 gelatine sheet (titanium grade)
4 egg yolks
70 g (2½ oz) white (granulated) sugar
Seeds of ½ vanilla bean
40 g (1½ oz) white chocolate
170 g (5¾ oz) mascarpone cheese
170 ml (5½ fl oz) thickened (whipping) cream

Pour the chardonnay into a saucepan. Bring to the boil and cook until the liquid has reduced by a third. Remove from the heat and set aside to cool.

Meanwhile, soak the gelatine in cold water to soften.

Whisk the egg yolks and sugar in a heatproof bowl, then whisk in the chardonnay and the vanilla seeds. Create a sabayon by whisking the mixture over a saucepan of simmering water until fluffy and glossy. Squeeze the excess water from the gelatine, add it to the sabayon and stir until dissolved and well combined. Add the white chocolate and stir until the mixture is smooth. Set aside to cool slightly.

Whisk the mascarpone and cream until medium peaks form. Fold the mixture into the sabayon and mix until well combined. Place in the fridge to set.

VERJUICE JELLY

250 ml (9 fl oz) verjuice
125 ml (4 fl oz) water
75 g (2½ oz) white (granulated) sugar
4 g (⅛ oz) konjac powder (see Note)

Put the verjuice, water, sugar and konjac in a saucepan and whisk to combine. Bring to the boil over medium heat.

Pour the verjuice mixture into a container and refrigerate until set.

NOTE: If you can't find konjac powder, replace it with the same quantity of agar.

FROZEN GREEN GRAPES

100 g (3½ oz) green grapes

Line a tray with baking paper. Slice the grapes into 5 mm (¼ inch) rounds and place them on the tray in a single layer. Place the tray in the freezer for 1–2 hours or until the grapes are frozen solid.

ASSEMBLY

Fennel fronds, to garnish
Linaria flowers, to garnish

Transfer the chardonnay mousse to a piping bag. Pipe the mousse into six small bowls and top with three or four small spoonfuls of the verjuice jelly. Arrange the frozen grapes on top of the jelly and garnish with the fennel and linaria flowers.

LEVEL

2

KICKIN' IT UP
A NOTCH

Let's step it up with swoon-worthy jar desserts and the perfect oozy lava cake

Level 2

ALL RIGHT!
NOW TO LEVEL-UP
AND THINK OUTSIDE
THE BOX BY ADDING
A LITTLE FLAIR TO
YOUR REPERTOIRE.

1

Whether you skipped Chapter 1 and decided to get right into this one or, better yet, if you tried some of those recipes and want to *challenge* yourself further, these dishes are perfect for *cooking fanatics.*

↓↓↓

2

Some of these recipes are favourites that are sold at KOI Dessert Bar, which you can try making at home. Lots of our creations look *stunning* but when you break down the recipes, they're not that difficult. They do take a bit of time and effort, but they are all *worth it* in the end.

3

Hopefully you'll find some new *tricks* to keep up your sleeve from this chapter and also some insight into new flavours. Some of these recipes are quite advanced and some are quite *fun and quirky* and won't take too much of your time, but they're all absolutely delicious.

WATERMELON JAR

This is the most refreshing dessert jar that we sell at KOI. It's quite filling and could almost be considered a healthy meal ... the watermelon and chia seeds are healthy, at least!

Watermelon jars are a perfect summer dessert when you're having a barbecue with friends. I'd even have one for breakfast. They're really not difficult to make – a few simple components and you're done. Of course, you don't have to make all the components, but if you do go to the effort, it's guaranteed to be a knockout.

BERRY CONSOMMÉ JELLY

300 ml (10½ fl oz) water
160 g (5½ oz) caster (superfine) sugar
Juice of ½ lemon
150 g (5½ oz) frozen strawberries
230 g (8 oz) frozen raspberries
4 gelatine sheets (titanium grade)
8–12 tinned lychees, halved
6 pinches of dried rose petals

Combine the water, sugar, lemon juice and berries in a saucepan. Bring to the boil over high heat, then reduce the heat to low and simmer for 20 minutes to reduce the liquid.

Meanwhile, soak the gelatine in cold water to soften.

Line a fine sieve with cheesecloth and place it over a smaller saucepan. Strain the berry mixture into the pan without agitation – don't push the liquid through or it will become cloudy. Bring the consommé to a simmer over medium heat, then remove from the heat. Squeeze the excess water from the softened gelatine, add it to the consommé and whisk until dissolved and well combined.

Pour 30 ml (1 fl oz) of the jelly into four to six 300 ml (10½ fl oz) jars or small bowls. Add four lychee halves and a pinch of rose petals to each jar. Place the jars in the fridge to set the jelly.

CHIA SEED SYRUP

45 g (1½ oz) chia seeds
300 ml (10½ fl oz) water
100 g (3½ oz) caster (superfine) sugar

Put the chia seeds in a heatproof bowl.

Stir the water and sugar together in a small saucepan. Bring to the boil over high heat, then pour the syrup over the chia seeds and mix to combine. Set aside for 10–15 minutes, then refrigerate until needed.

CRÈME PÂTISSIÈRE

500 ml (17 fl oz) full-cream milk
4 egg yolks
110 g (3¾ oz) caster (superfine) sugar
40 g (1½ oz) cornflour (cornstarch)

Pour the milk into a saucepan and bring it to a simmer.

Meanwhile, whisk the egg yolks and sugar until fluffy, then stir in the cornflour until the mixture is well combined and forms a paste-like consistency.

Whisk the hot milk into the egg yolk mixture, then pour the mixture back into the pan and whisk over medium heat until it has thickened to a very firm custard-like consistency. Immediately use the hot crème pâtissière to make the lychee diplomat cream (see page 73). →

LYCHEE DIPLOMAT CREAM

1 gelatine sheet (titanium grade)
1 quantity crème pâtissière (*page 70*)
35 g (1¼ oz) caster (superfine) sugar
50 ml (1¾ fl oz) Soho (lychee-
    flavoured spirit)
15 ml (½ fl oz) rosewater
300 ml (10½ fl oz) thickened
    (whipping) cream

Soak the gelatine in cold water to soften.

Pour the hot crème pâtissière into a jug. Squeeze the excess water from the softened gelatine and add it to the jug. Add the sugar, Soho and rosewater and, using an immersion blender, blend until the mixture is completely smooth. Transfer the mixture to a bowl and refrigerate for 30–45 minutes or until cool.

Whisk the cream until medium peaks form, then fold it through the crème pâtissière mixture. Place in the fridge until needed.

SABLÉ CRUMBLE

125 g (4½ oz) unsalted butter,
    softened
190 g (6¾ oz) almond meal
160 g (5½ oz) caster (superfine) sugar
65 g (2¼ oz) plain (all-purpose) flour
3 g (⅛ oz) salt

Preheat the oven to 170°C (340°F). Line a baking tray with baking paper.

Combine the butter, almond meal, sugar, flour and salt in a mixer fitted with the paddle attachment. Mix on medium–low speed until a dough is formed.

Evenly spread the dough over the baking tray and bake for 15–20 minutes or until golden brown.

Allow the sablé to cool, then transfer it to a food processor and pulse until crumbled. (You can also use your hands to crush the sablé.) Store the crumble in an airtight container until needed.

ASSEMBLY

½ watermelon, diced
250 g (9 oz) strawberries, sliced
    into rounds
Dried rose petals, for sprinkling
Micro mint, to garnish

Spoon 2 tablespoons of the chia seed syrup on top of the jelly in each jar. Top with a layer of the diced watermelon.

Transfer the lychee diplomat cream to a piping bag and pipe it into the jars so they are three-quarters full. Place the jars in the fridge to set for at least 10–15 minutes.

Divide the sablé crumble among the jars. Arrange four strawberry rounds in each jar. Sprinkle a pinch of dried rose petals into each jar and add some mint. Serve immediately or refrigerate until serving.

A SLICE OF IRISH CREAM

I love, love, love Baileys! My earliest memory of the classic Irish cream liqueur is enjoying it with a scoop of ice cream.

This is one of our simpler slice cakes as the layers aren't too difficult to make. When we do have multiple layers in a slice cake, it takes forever to build each component and then layer each one. It seriously takes hours.

This slice cake is best enjoyed with coffee for brunch or in the early afternoon. The velvet-soft mousse, chewy brownie and crunchy sablé are such a joyful textural experience to eat and you can distinguish all of the beautifully balanced flavours.

SABLÉ BASE

250 g (9 oz) unsalted butter, softened
250 g (9 oz) almond meal
230 g (8 oz) caster (superfine) sugar
200 g (7 oz) plain (all-purpose) flour
5 g (⅛ oz) salt
2 egg yolks
70 g (2½ oz) cocoa butter

Preheat the oven to 170°C (340°F). Line two baking trays with baking paper and place a 20 cm (8 inch) square stainless steel pastry frame on one of the trays.

Combine the butter, almond meal, sugar, flour and salt in a mixer fitted with the paddle attachment. Add the egg yolks and mix until a dough is formed.

Evenly spread the dough over the baking tray and bake for 15–20 minutes or until golden brown. Allow to cool, then transfer the sablé to a food processor and process until crumbs are formed. Transfer the crumbs to a bowl.

Melt the cocoa butter in a heatproof bowl in the microwave or over a saucepan of simmering water, then add it to the sablé crumbs and mix until combined. Spread the crumb mix inside the pastry frame and press it down with an offset palette knife to make it completely level. Place the base in the fridge to set.

CHOCOLATE BROWNIE

80 g (2¾ oz) unsalted butter
65 g (2¼ oz) dark chocolate
95 g (3¼ oz) caster (superfine) sugar
25 g (1 oz) plain (all-purpose) flour
25 g (1 oz) dark cocoa powder
2 g (¹⁄₁₆ oz) baking powder
2 eggs

Preheat the oven to 170°C (340°F). Line a 15 x 30 cm (6 x 12 inch) shallow baking tray with baking paper.

Combine the butter and chocolate in a glass bowl and microwave on high in 45–60 second bursts, stirring in between, until completely melted. Alternatively, combine the butter and chocolate in a heatproof bowl and stir over a saucepan of simmering water until melted.

Combine the sugar, flour, cocoa and baking powder in a mixer fitted with the paddle attachment. Turn the mixer to medium–low speed and slowly pour in the chocolate mixture. Mix until completely combined. Scrape down the side of the bowl, then turn the mixer to low and add the eggs, one at a time, ensuring the first one is completely combined before adding the second. →

Pour the brownie mixture onto the baking tray and bake for 15–20 minutes or until a skewer inserted into the centre comes out with a few moist crumbs stuck to it. Leave the brownie on the tray until completely cool, then transfer it to an airtight container until needed.

NOTE: You can cut this deliciously rich brownie into squares and serve it as is or with a scoop of your favourite ice cream.

HAZELNUT GANACHE

200 ml (7 fl oz) thickened (whipping) cream
75 g (2½ oz) dark chocolate
225 g (8 oz) milk chocolate
150 g (5½ oz) hazelnut praline paste (see Note)

Pour the cream into a small saucepan and bring to the boil over medium heat.

Meanwhile, combine the dark chocolate, milk chocolate and praline paste in a heatproof bowl. Pour in the hot cream and stir until melted. Use an immersion blender to blend the ganache for 1–2 minutes or until it is completely smooth.

Pour the ganache onto the sablé base and use an offset palette knife to level it.

Roughly break the brownie into pieces and arrange them on top of the ganache, gently pressing them down. Set aside while you prepare the Baileys mousse.

NOTE: You'll find praline paste in specialty food stores. You can also use the peanut & hazelnut praline paste from page 117 or buy a chocolate hazelnut spread (such as Nutella).

BAILEYS MOUSSE

3 gelatine sheets (titanium grade)
150 ml (5½ fl oz) full-cream milk
5 g (⅛ oz) freeze-dried coffee granules
40 g (1½ oz) egg yolks
40 g (1½ oz) caster (superfine) sugar
105 g (3½ oz) milk chocolate
30 g (1 oz) dark chocolate
55 ml (1¾ fl oz) thickened (whipping) cream
105 g (3½ oz) mascarpone cheese
60 ml (2 fl oz) Baileys Irish Cream liqueur
10 ml (¼ fl oz) Kahlúa coffee liqueur

Soak the gelatine in cold water to soften.

Combine the milk and coffee granules in a small saucepan and bring to the boil over high heat.

Meanwhile, whisk the egg yolks and sugar in a heatproof bowl until combined. Whisk in half of the hot milk mixture, then pour the mixture back into the pan and cook over medium heat, stirring constantly with a spatula, until the anglaise thickens and reaches 85°C (185°F) on a sugar thermometer. Remove from the heat. Squeeze the excess water from the softened gelatine, add it to the pan and stir until dissolved and well combined.

Combine the milk and dark chocolate in a bowl and, using a fine sieve, strain the anglaise into the bowl. Whisk until completely combined, then leave the mixture to cool to 40°C (104°F).

Fold the cream into the chocolate mixture, followed by the mascarpone and then the liqueurs. Pour the mousse into the pastry frame on top of the brownie and use an offset palette knife to level it. Place in the freezer for 1–2 hours or until firm. →

COFFEE JELLY

2 gelatine sheets (titanium grade)
150 ml (5 fl oz) water
75 g (2½ oz) caster (superfine) sugar
75 ml (2¼ fl oz) espresso

Soak the gelatine in cold water to soften.

Meanwhile, combine the water and sugar in a small saucepan and bring to the boil. Remove the pan from the heat.

Squeeze the excess water from the softened gelatine, add it to the pan and stir until dissolved and well combined. Stir in the espresso, then set aside to cool completely.

ASSEMBLY

Pour the cooled coffee jelly mixture into the pastry frame on top of the Baileys mousse and refrigerate for 15–20 minutes or until completely set.

Gently warm the outside of the pastry frame with a blowtorch to help release it. Warm a long sharp knife in hot water, then wipe the knife and slice the cake in half to make two 10 x 20 cm (4 x 8 inch) slabs. Using a ruler as a guide, cut each slab into 4 x 10 cm (1½ x 4 inch) slices, heating and wiping the knife blade before each cut. Transfer to the fridge to thaw before serving.

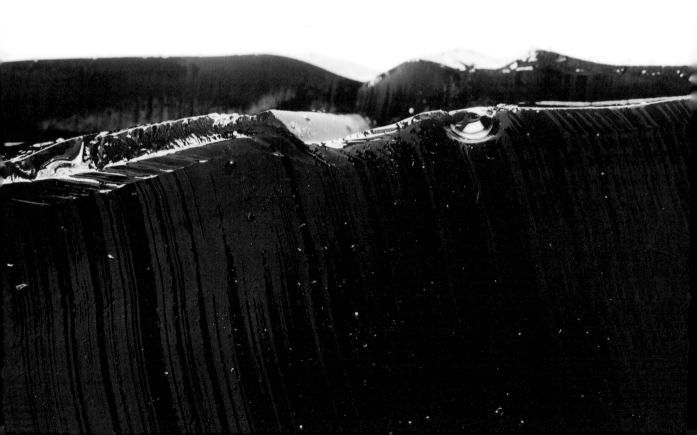

MR GREY

This dessert is pretty on the palate. You'll know what I mean when you take a spoonful – it's light, fresh, fruity and punchy, with a textural experience that is almost seductive. It will leave you wanting more and more, just like Mr Grey – and the name is obviously inspired by the tea used in the recipe. This is actually one of my favourites and a favourite at the shop, too!

FRENCH EARL GREY CRÈME PÂTISSIÈRE

500 ml (17 fl oz) full-cream milk
10 g (¼ oz) French Earl Grey tea
4 egg yolks
110 g (3¾ oz) caster (superfine) sugar
40 g (1½ oz) cornflour (cornstarch)

Combine the milk and tea in a saucepan and bring to a simmer.

Meanwhile, whisk the egg yolks and sugar until fluffy, then stir in the cornflour until the mixture is well combined and forms a paste-like consistency.

Whisk the hot milk tea into the egg yolk mixture, then strain the mixture back into the pan. Whisk the mixture over medium heat until it has thickened to a very firm custard-like consistency. Immediately use the hot crème pâtissière to make the French Earl Grey diplomat cream (see below).

FRENCH EARL GREY DIPLOMAT CREAM

1 gelatine sheet (titanium grade)
350 g (12 oz) white chocolate
1 quantity crème pâtissière
 (see above)
300 ml (10½ fl oz) thickened
 (whipping) cream

Soak the gelatine in cold water to soften.

Put the white chocolate in a jug and add the hot crème pâtissière. Squeeze the excess water from the softened gelatine and add it to the jug. Using an immersion blender, blend until the mixture is completely smooth. Transfer the mixture to a bowl and refrigerate for 30–45 minutes or until cool.

Whisk the cream until medium peaks form, then fold it through the crème pâtissière mixture.

Divide the diplomat cream among six 300 ml (10½ fl oz) jars or small bowls and place in the fridge until needed.

YUZU JELLY

125 ml (4 fl oz) yuzu juice
90 g (3¼ oz) white (granulated)
 sugar
90 ml (3 fl oz) water
4 g (⅛ oz) agar

Combine the yuzu juice, sugar and water in a small saucepan and whisk in the agar. Bring the mixture to the boil over high heat and allow it to boil for 10 seconds, then remove the pan from the heat.

Pour the mixture into a container and refrigerate for 10–15 minutes or until set. →

STRAWBERRY CRUMBLE

100 g (3½ oz) white chocolate
30 g (1 oz) maltodextrin
60 g (2¼ oz) freeze-dried strawberry
  slices, crushed

Melt the white chocolate in a heatproof bowl in the microwave or over a saucepan of simmering water.

Slowly whisk in the maltodextrin, one spoonful at a time. The mixture should resemble a very light and soft crumble.

Whisk the crushed strawberries into the chocolate mixture. Transfer to a container and store in the fridge until needed.

ASSEMBLY

12 strawberries, quartered
9 lychees, quartered
Micro mint, to garnish

Spoon the strawberrry crumble over the diplomat cream in each jar. Arrange the strawberry and lychee quarters on top.

Remove the yuzu jelly from the container and cut it into 1 cm (½ inch) cubes. Add seven cubes of jelly to each jar, then garnish with the micro mint.

Return the jars to the fridge if you're not serving them straight away.

CHOCOLATE LAVA S'MORES

Ahh, the infamous lava cake! Props to the legend who invented this iconic French classic that was originally known as *Chocolat coulant*, which translates as 'flowing chocolate'. If you think lava cake is just undercooked cake, think again. Sure, it's easier to make it that way, but eating doughy, eggy, floury, undercooked cake simply for the sake of that 'ooze' is not cool! The proper way (and I believe the only way) to make lava cake is with a velvety, molten ganache centre. My s'mores version has a touch of oomph without being overly sickening. I've replaced caster sugar with palm sugar in the cake batter, dialling the sweetness right down and making it incredibly moreish.

You'll need to start this recipe about 4 to 5 hours in advance, unless you have a badass freezer that can speed up the freezing of the ganache.

GANACHE CENTRES

150 ml (5 fl oz) thickened (whipping) cream
150 g (5½ oz) 55% dark chocolate
15 g (½ oz) unsalted butter

Pour the cream into a small saucepan and bring it to a simmer.

Put the chocolate in a heatproof jug. Pour in the hot cream and, using an immersion blender, blend in the chocolate. Add the butter and blend until glossy and smooth.

Pour the ganache into four 5 cm (2 inch) diameter silicone mini muffin moulds. Place in the freezer for 4–5 hours or until frozen solid.

LAVA CAKES

150 g (5½ oz) unsalted butter, plus extra for greasing
150 g (5½ oz) 60% dark chocolate
65 g (2¼ oz) dark palm sugar (jaggery)
3 eggs
3 egg yolks
40 g (1½ oz) plain (all-purpose) flour
Pinch of salt

Combine the butter, chocolate and palm sugar in a heatproof bowl over a saucepan of simmering water and stir occasionally until melted and combined.

Whisk in the eggs and egg yolks. Add the flour and salt and whisk until the batter is thick and smooth. Transfer to a bowl and refrigerate for at least 30 minutes.

Preheat the oven to 170°C (340°F). Grease four 7 cm (2¾ inch) cake rings with butter and tightly wrap the bottoms with foil to create a base, then grease the foil bases. Place the cake rings on a baking tray. Alternatively, grease four 8.5 cm (3¼ inch) ramekins with butter.

Transfer the chilled batter to a piping bag and half-fill the greased moulds, then place a frozen ganache round in the centre of the batter. Make sure the ganache is sitting directly in the middle of the batter. Pipe more batter over the ganache until the moulds are three-quarters full. *See photographs on page 86.*

Bake the lava cakes for 18–20 minutes. Meanwhile, prepare the Italian meringue (see page 87).

Allow the cooked cakes to cool for a few minutes, then run a small knife around the edge of each one to loosen it and turn it out. ➜

LAVA CAKES: Tightly wrap the bottom of each greased cake ring with foil to create a base.

Pipe the chilled lava cake batter into the greased cake rings until they are about half full.

Use a skewer to help place a frozen ganache round in each mould, ensuring it is sitting directly in the middle of the batter.

Pipe more of the lava cake batter over the frozen ganache round until the cake ring is three-quarters full.

ITALIAN MERINGUE

180 g (6 oz) white (granulated) sugar
50 ml (1¾ fl oz) water
90 g (3¼ oz) egg whites

We've got left-over egg whites, so we may as well turn them into meringue …

Combine the sugar and water in a small saucepan over low heat. Once the syrup reaches 100°C (212°F) on a sugar thermometer, put the egg whites in a mixer fitted with the whisk attachment and turn the speed to medium–low.

As soon as the syrup reaches 118°C (244°F), remove the pan from the heat, turn the mixer to medium speed and slowly pour the syrup onto the egg whites in a thin stream down the side of the bowl. Turn the mixer to full speed and whisk until the bowl has completely cooled down.

ASSEMBLY

Freeze-dried mandarin segments
Grated citrus zest, to garnish
  (optional)
Edible flowers, to garnish (optional)
Ice cream of your choice, to serve

Stand each lava cake on a serving plate. Place a spoonful of the meringue on the side of each cake. Work it upwards, making little peaks with the back of the spoon. Use a blowtorch to brown the meringue.

Lightly brown the freeze-dried mandarin segments with the blowtorch.

Garnish each lava cake with the mandarin segments, some citrus zest and edible flowers, if using. Top it all off with some ice cream and cut into that bad boy to see it ooze.

NOTES: You can replace the freeze-dried mandarin segments with fresh orange segments. Use any left-over ganache to make amazing hot chocolate or heat it and pour it over the ice cream alongside the lava cakes.

TIRAMISU JAR

This is one of the favourites at KOI. It's Mum's recipe and I remember the days when she was selling her handmade tiramisu. They weren't the typical layered cakes in a tray but beautiful whole cakes, so you can imagine how fragile they were. I was the delivery boy back then and one day I was doing a drop-off on the way to uni. I had about five tiramisu cakes on board, but I was late and I didn't slow down for a speed bump. Oh my ... I'll just say I died at that moment. All of the cakes were smashed. So here's our jar version – it's smash-free and travel safe, with 100 per cent satisfaction.

COFFEE JELLY

2 gelatine sheets (titanium grade)
100 ml (3½ fl oz) espresso
65 ml (2 fl oz) water
65 g (2¼ oz) white (granulated) sugar
30 ml (1 fl oz) Kahlúa coffee liqueur

Soak the gelatine in cold water to soften.

Combine the espresso, water, sugar and Kahlúa in a small saucepan. Squeeze the excess water from the softened gelatine and add it to the pan. Stir over low heat until the mixture is well combined and the gelatine has dissolved.

Pour the jelly into a container and refrigerate for 2–3 hours or until set.

SOAKED COFFEE SPONGE

150 g (5½ oz) white (granulated) sugar
150 ml (5 fl oz) water
60 ml (2 fl oz) espresso
20 ml (½ fl oz) Kahlúa coffee liqueur
150 g (5½ oz) sponge finger biscuits
75 g (2½ oz) dark chocolate

Combine the sugar, water, espresso and Kahlúa in a saucepan and bring to a simmer. Remove from the heat and set aside to cool to room temperature.

Combine the sponge finger biscuits and chocolate in a food processor and blend until slightly crushed, but not too fine.

Add enough of the coffee syrup to the crumble to make it damp.

Spoon the soaked sponge mixture into eight 300 ml (10½ fl oz) jars or small bowls. Place the jars in the fridge until needed. ➜

TIRAMISU MOUSSE

1 gelatine sheet (titanium grade)
1 egg white
155 g (5½ oz) white (granulated)
    sugar
5 egg yolks
120 ml (3¾ fl oz) espresso
30 ml (1 fl oz) Kahlúa coffee liqueur
500 g (1 lb 2 oz) mascarpone cheese
100 ml (3½ fl oz) single (pure) cream

Soak the gelatine in cold water to soften.

Meanwhile, combine the egg white and 80 g (2¾ oz) of the sugar in a mixer fitted with the whisk attachment and whisk until stiff peaks form.

Combine the egg yolks and the remaining 75 g (2½ oz) of sugar in a heatproof bowl over a saucepan of simmering water. Whisk until fluffy to create a sabayon. Whisk in the espresso and Kahlúa. Squeeze the excess water from the softened gelatine, add it to the sabayon and stir until dissolved and well combined. Fold the meringue into the sabayon.

Combine the mascarpone and cream in a bowl and whisk until medium peaks form. Fold the mixture into the sabayon.

Transfer the mousse to a piping bag and pipe it into the jars on top of the sponge mixture until the jars are three-quarters full. Place in the fridge to set.

HAZELNUT SPONGE

4 eggs
1 egg white
20 g (¾ oz) plain (all-purpose) flour
30 g (1 oz) white (granulated) sugar
60 g (2¼ oz) hazelnut praline paste
    or chocolate hazelnut spread
    (such as Nutella)

Use a skewer to poke five holes in the base of a microwave-safe takeaway coffee cup.

Put all of the sponge ingredients in a jug and blend with an immersion blender until combined.

Strain the mixture into a cream whipper and charge twice with N2O. Siphon the mixture into the cup until half full. Microwave the sponge on high for 45 seconds or until the top is dry to the touch. Allow the sponge to cool upside down on a wire rack. *See photographs on page 142.*

ASSEMBLY

Dark cocoa powder, for dusting

Lightly dust the mousse in the jars with the cocoa powder.

Break the hazelnut sponge into chunks and divide it among the jars.

Cut the coffee jelly into 1 cm (½ inch) cubes. Add several jelly cubes to each jar.

RUBY RASPBERRY & ROSE TART

START THIS RECIPE
A DAY AHEAD

This gorgeous, intense red tart is full of fragrance and texture. It does take a bit of effort to arrange the berries in an orderly manner, but it adds a note of elegance.

RUBY CRÉMEUX

½ gelatine sheet (titanium grade)
50 ml (1¾ fl oz) full-cream milk
150 ml (5 fl oz) single (pure) cream
100 g (3½ oz) raspberry purée
2 eggs
10 g (¼ oz) white (granulated) sugar
200 g (7 oz) ruby chocolate

Soak the gelatine in cold water to soften.

Combine the milk, cream and raspberry purée in a saucepan and bring to the boil.

Meanwhile, whisk the eggs and sugar in a heatproof bowl until fluffy. Whisk in the hot milk mixture, then pour the mixture back into the pan and cook until it reaches 83°C (181°F) on a sugar thermometer. Squeeze the excess water from the softened gelatine, add it to the pan with the ruby chocolate and whisk until smooth. Strain the crémeux into a container and refrigerate overnight.

FRENCH EARL GREY TART SHELL

375 g (13 oz) plain (all-purpose) flour, plus extra for dusting
80 g (2¾ oz) white (granulated) sugar
200 g (7 oz) chilled unsalted butter, cubed
6 g (⅛ oz) French Earl Grey tea, ground to a fine powder
1 egg
1 egg yolk
50 g (1¾ oz) white chocolate

Preheat the oven to 170°C (340°F). Place a 20 x 2 cm (8 x ¾ inch) perforated tart ring on a baking tray lined with baking paper.

Combine the flour, sugar, butter and ground tea in a mixer fitted with the paddle attachment. Mix until a sandy texture is formed. Slowly add the egg and yolk and mix until a dough is formed. Wrap in plastic wrap and refrigerate for 30 minutes.

Roll out the chilled dough on a lightly floured surface to a thickness of 3–5 mm (⅛–¼ inch). Drape the dough over the tart ring and tuck in the edges, cutting off the excess. Prick the centre of the tart shell with a skewer a few times. Line the shell with baking paper and fill with baking beads or uncooked rice. Blind bake the shell for 15 minutes. Remove the paper and beads or rice and bake for a further 15 minutes or until golden. Set aside to cool.

Melt the white chocolate in a heatproof bowl in the microwave or over a saucepan of simmering water. Coat the inside of the tart shell with the melted chocolate.

BERRY COMPOTE

100 ml (3½ fl oz) rosé wine
150 g (5½ oz) raspberries, halved
150 g (5½ oz) strawberries, quartered
85 ml (2¾ fl oz) water
50 ml (1¾ fl oz) lemon juice
80 g (2¾ oz) white (granulated) sugar
4.5 g (⅛ oz) pectin NH powder

Combine the rosé, berries, water and lemon juice in a saucepan. Cook over medium–high heat for 15–20 minutes or until the berries have broken down.

Whisk the sugar and pectin together, then whisk it into the berry mixture and bring to the boil. Remove the pan from the heat. Transfer the berry compote to a container and place in the fridge until needed. →

ROSEWATER JELLY

50 ml (1¾ fl oz) rosewater
100 ml (3½ fl oz) water
50 g (1¾ oz) white (granulated) sugar
2 g (¹⁄₁₆ oz) agar

Combine the rosewater, water, sugar and agar in a saucepan and whisk over high heat until boiling.

Transfer the jelly mixture to a small tray or container. Place in the fridge for 10–15 minutes or until set.

ASSEMBLY

10 strawberries, cut into eighths
16 raspberries
Dried rose petals, for sprinkling

Transfer the berry compote to a piping bag and pipe it into the tart shell as shown below, leaving a 1 cm (½ inch) gap from the top edge.

Transfer the ruby crémeux to a piping bag. Pipe a 1 cm (½ inch) thick layer of crémeux on top of the berry compote as shown. Place in the fridge to set for 15 minutes.

Cut the rosewater jelly into 5 mm (¼ inch) cubes.

Arrange the strawberry pieces and raspberries on top of the ruby crémeux. Scatter spoonfuls of the rosewater jelly cubes on top of the berries and garnish with the dried rose petals.

ASSEMBLY: Pipe the berry compote into the chocolate-coated tart shell, leaving a gap at the top.

Pipe a thick, even layer of the ruby crémeux so that it completely covers the berry compote.

STRAWBERRIES & CREAM

START THIS RECIPE
A DAY AHEAD

This isn't the craziest flavour pairing, but it isn't the usual strawberries and cream, either. Adding elderflower and lemongrass oil into the mix really elevates the beautiful fragrance that strawberries have to offer. It's a stunning dessert that looks impressive and tastes even more so. It's also a timeless dish that I never get tired of – it's just so damn tasty.

LEMONGRASS OIL

2 lemongrass stems
100 ml (3½ fl oz) grapeseed oil

Chop the lemongrass as finely as possible, then place in a saucepan with the grapeseed oil. Bring to a simmer over low heat, then cook for 30 minutes or until fragrant. Remove from the heat and set aside until cooled to 80°C (176°F).

Transfer the mixture to a blender and blend for 30 seconds. Store in a jar overnight, then strain the oil.

ELDERFLOWER & VANILLA PANNA COTTA

2 gelatine sheets (titanium grade)
250 ml (9 fl oz) full-cream milk
50 ml (1¾ fl oz) elderflower syrup
50 g (1¾ oz) caster (superfine) sugar
Seeds of 1 vanilla bean
250 ml (9 fl oz) thickened (whipping) cream

Soak the gelatine in cold water to soften.

Combine the milk, elderflower syrup, sugar and vanilla seeds in a saucepan and bring to a simmer. Remove the pan from the heat. Squeeze the excess water from the softened gelatine, add it to the pan and whisk until dissolved and well combined. Whisk in the cream, then strain the mixture into a jug.

Pour 100 ml (3½ fl oz) of the panna cotta mixture into six deep bowls. Place in the fridge for at least 3–4 hours to set.

STRAWBERRY GRANITA

500 g (1 lb 2 oz) strawberries, quartered
500 ml (17 fl oz) water
100 g (3½ oz) caster (superfine) sugar
Juice of ½ lemon
Seeds of ½ vanilla bean

Place the strawberries in a saucepan with the water, sugar, lemon juice and vanilla seeds. Cook over medium heat for 20–30 minutes or until the strawberries begin to soften and turn pale.

Strain the mixture into a container or tray, discarding the strawberry pulp. Set aside to cool, then place in the freezer for 1 hour. Scrape any frozen mixture with a fork, then return to the freezer. Repeat the scraping and freezing process until you have an intense red strawberry granita. →

MILK ICE CREAM

450 ml (16 fl oz) thickened
   (whipping) cream
300 ml (10½ fl oz) full-cream milk
50 g (1¾ oz) liquid glucose
5 egg yolks
110 g (3¾ oz) white (granulated)
   sugar
75 g (2½ oz) full-cream milk powder

Combine the cream, milk and glucose in a saucepan and bring to a simmer.

Meanwhile, whisk the egg yolks and sugar until fluffy, then whisk in the hot cream mixture. Pour the mixture back into the pan and stir over medium heat until it reaches 85°C (185°F) on a sugar thermometer.

Strain the mixture into a jug. Using an immersion blender, blend in the milk powder until dissolved. Set aside to cool completely.

Churn the mixture in an ice-cream maker until firm, then place in the freezer until ready to serve.

LYCHEE JELLY

200 ml (7 fl oz) lychee juice
20 ml (½ fl oz) Soho
   (lychee-flavoured spirit)
25 g (1 oz) caster (superfine) sugar
¼ teaspoon citric acid
2.5 g (¹⁄₁₆ oz) agar

Put the lychee juice, Soho, sugar, citric acid and agar in a saucepan and whisk until combined. Bring to the boil, then pour the mixture into a heatproof container and allow it to cool. Place in the fridge until completely set.

Cut the jelly into 1 cm (½ inch) cubes.

ASSEMBLY

Bronze fennel fronds, to garnish

Spoon the granita over the panna cotta, then scatter the lychee jelly cubes over the top. Add a spoonful of the milk ice cream.

Using a spoon, drizzle the lemongrass oil over the ice cream and garnish with the fennel fronds. Serve immediately.

SERVES 8

BLACKFOREST JAR

Here's another classic turned into a jar dessert, with layers similar to a trifle. It's such a fun way to enjoy the dessert without having to commit to a full cake. The recipe isn't completely traditional, but it's true to a blackforest cake with a bit of a twist. And it's a total textural experience, with the traditional sponge being replaced with a brownie and some homemade jellies added into the mix.

BERRY CONSOMMÉ JELLY

300 ml (10½ fl oz) water
160 g (5½ oz) caster (superfine) sugar
Juice of ½ lemon
300 g (10½ oz) frozen mixed berries
1 gelatine sheet (titanium grade)

Combine the water, sugar, lemon juice and berries in a saucepan. Bring to the boil over high heat, then reduce the heat to low and simmer for 20 minutes to reduce the liquid.

Meanwhile, soak the gelatine in cold water to soften.

Line a fine sieve with cheesecloth and place it over a smaller saucepan. Strain the berry mixture into the pan without agitation – do not push the liquid through or it will become cloudy. Bring the consommé to a simmer over medium heat, then remove from the heat. Squeeze the excess water from the softened gelatine, add it to the consommé and whisk until dissolved and well combined.

Pour 30 ml (1 fl oz) of the jelly into eight 300 ml (10½ fl oz) jars or small bowls and place in the fridge to set.

CHOCOLATE BROWNIE

250 g (9 oz) unsalted butter
200 g (7 oz) dark chocolate
300 g (10½ oz) caster (superfine) sugar
80 g (2¾ oz) plain (all-purpose) flour
80 g (2¾ oz) dark cocoa powder
2 g (¹⁄₁₆ oz) baking powder
4 eggs

Preheat the oven to 170°C (340°F). Line a 20 cm (8 inch) square cake tin with baking paper.

Combine the butter and chocolate in a glass bowl and microwave on high in 45–60 second bursts, stirring in between, until completely melted. Alternatively, combine the butter and chocolate in a heatproof bowl and stir over a saucepan of simmering water until melted.

Combine the sugar, flour, cocoa and baking powder in a mixer fitted with the paddle attachment. Turn the mixer to medium–low speed and slowly pour in the chocolate mixture. Mix until completely combined. Scrape down the side of the bowl, then turn the mixer to low and add the eggs, one at a time, ensuring they are completely combined before adding the next one.

Pour the brownie mixture into the cake tin and bake for 15–20 minutes or until a skewer inserted into the centre comes out with a few moist crumbs stuck to it. Leave the brownie in the tin until completely cool, then transfer it to an airtight container until needed. ➔

CHERRY COMPOTE

500 g (1 lb 2 oz) fresh or frozen
    pitted cherries
95 g (3¼ oz) caster (superfine) sugar
Grated zest and juice of 1 lemon
1 cinnamon stick
1 star anise
12 g (¼ oz) cornflour (cornstarch)
20 ml (½ fl oz) water
5 ml (⅛ fl oz) kirsch (cherry liqueur)

Combine the cherries, sugar, lemon zest, lemon juice, cinnamon stick and star anise in a saucepan. Bring to the boil over high heat.

Reduce the heat to medium–low and simmer for 10–15 minutes or until the cherries have softened and the mixture has thickened to a jam-like consistency.

Combine the cornflour and water in a small bowl to make a slurry. Whisk the slurry into the cherry mixture, increase the heat to medium and bring to the boil.

Pour the cherry compote into a deep tray and set it aside to cool. Remove the cinnamon stick and star anise, then stir in the kirsch.

NOTE: If you're concerned about the alcohol in the kirsch, add the kirsch when you first add the cherries to the pan so that the alcohol will cook out.

CRÈME PÂTISSIÈRE

500 ml (17 fl oz) full-cream milk
4 egg yolks
110 g (3¾ oz) caster (superfine) sugar
40 g (1½ oz) cornflour (cornstarch)

Pour the milk into a saucepan and bring it to a simmer.

Meanwhile, whisk the egg yolks and sugar until fluffy, then stir in the cornflour until the mixture is well combined and forms a paste-like consistency.

Whisk the hot milk into the egg yolk mixture, then pour the mixture back into the pan and whisk over medium heat until it has thickened to a very firm custard-like consistency. Immediately use the hot crème pâtissière to make the blackforest diplomat cream (see below).

BLACKFOREST DIPLOMAT CREAM

1 gelatine sheet (titanium grade)
1 quantity crème pâtissière
    (*see above*)
35 g (1¼ oz) caster (superfine) sugar
40 ml (1¼ fl oz) kirsch
    (cherry liqueur)
10 ml (¼ fl oz) dark rum
300 ml (10½ fl oz) thickened
    (whipping) cream

Soak the gelatine in cold water to soften.

Pour the hot crème pâtissière into a jug. Squeeze the excess water from the softened gelatine and add it to the jug, along with the sugar, kirsch and rum. Using an immersion blender, blend until the mixture is completely smooth. Transfer the mixture to a bowl and refrigerate for 30–45 minutes or until cool.

Whisk the cream until medium peaks form, then fold it through the crème pâtissière mixture. Place in the fridge until needed. →

CHOCOLATE SABLÉ CRUMBS

125 g (4½ oz) unsalted butter, softened
190 g (6¾ oz) almond meal
160 g (5½ oz) caster (superfine) sugar
65 g (2¼ oz) plain (all-purpose) flour
15 g (½ oz) dark cocoa powder
2.5 g (¹⁄₁₆ oz) salt

Preheat the oven to 170°C (340°F). Line a baking tray with baking paper.

Combine the butter, almond meal, sugar, flour, cocoa and salt in a mixer fitted with the paddle attachment. Mix on medium–low speed until a dough is formed.

Evenly spread the dough over the baking tray and bake for 15–20 minutes or until golden brown.

Allow the sablé to cool, then transfer it to a food processor and pulse until crumbled. (You can also use your hands to crush the sablé.) Store the crumbs in an airtight container until needed.

ASSEMBLY

200 g (7 oz) dark chocolate, roughly chopped
20 cherries, pitted and halved
Fennel fronds, to garnish
Linaria flowers, to garnish

Roughly break the brownie into pieces. Spoon two or three large spoonfuls of the brownie pieces on top of the jelly in each jar.

Divide the chopped dark chocolate among the jars, then add a large spoonful of the cherry compote to each jar.

Transfer the blackforest diplomat cream to a jug or piping bag and pour or pipe it into each jar until they are three-quarters full. Place the jars in the fridge for 10–15 minutes or until set.

Divide the chocolate sablé crumbs among the jars. Garnish the jars with the cherries, fennel and linaria flowers.

TROPICAL PANNA COTTA JAR

Panna cotta is one of the first desserts I made back when I was fourteen, so this is basically the very first signature dessert of mine! It's derived from the Italian classic and paired with tropical ingredients. At first sight the flavour pairings aren't that special, but a few little touches, such as lime and saffron, go a long way to making this a pretty and unique dessert.

PASSIONFRUIT CURD

200 ml (7 fl oz) strained fresh passionfruit juice
130 g (4½ oz) unsalted butter
8 eggs
20 g (¾ oz) white (granulated) sugar

Combine the passionfruit juice and butter in a saucepan. Cook over medium heat until simmering.

Meanwhile, whisk the eggs and sugar in a heatproof bowl until fluffy. Whisk in the hot passionfruit mixture. Place the bowl over a saucepan of simmering water and cook, stirring once every couple of minutes, until the mixture has thickened.

Transfer the hot curd mixture into a jug and blend with an immersion blender. Pass the curd through a fine sieve and place in the fridge for a few hours or preferably overnight.

COCONUT PANNA COTTA

4 gelatine sheets (titanium grade)
350 ml (12 fl oz) full-cream milk
150 g (5½ oz) white (granulated) sugar
½ teaspoon salt
250 ml (9 fl oz) single (pure) cream
400 ml (14 fl oz) coconut milk

Soak the gelatine in cold water to soften.

Meanwhile, combine the milk, sugar and salt in a saucepan. Gently heat until simmering, ensuring the sugar and salt are dissolved. Squeeze the excess water from the softened gelatine, add it to the pan and stir until dissolved and well combined. Stir in the cream and coconut milk.

Pour the panna cotta mixture into four 300 ml (10½ fl oz) jars or small bowls and refrigerate for 4 hours or until set.

MANGO GEL

300 g (10½ oz) mango purée
50 g (1¾ oz) white (granulated) sugar
Juice of 1 lime
3.7 g (⅛ oz) agar

Combine the mango purée, sugar and lime juice in a blender. Blend in the agar. Pour the mixture into a saucepan over high heat. Once the mixture comes to the boil, allow it to boil for 10 seconds, then remove the pan from the heat.

Pour the mixture into a container and refrigerate for 10–15 minutes or until set.

Using an immersion blender, blend the jelly until smooth, then pass it through a fine sieve. Transfer the gel to a piping bag and place in the fridge until needed. →

COCONUT SAGO

500 ml (17 fl oz) water
100 g (3½ oz) sago pearls
50 ml (1¾ fl oz) coconut milk,
    plus extra if needed
Palm sugar (jaggery), to taste

Pour the water into a saucepan and bring to the boil. Add the sago pearls and cook over medium heat for 10 minutes or until only a small white dot remains on the pearls. Strain the sago and run it under cold water.

Combine the sago and coconut milk in a container. Stir in grated palm sugar, to taste. Place in the fridge until needed. If the sago soaks up too much liquid and dries up, add some coconut milk to loosen the mixture.

CARAMELISED PINEAPPLE

400 g (14 oz) diced pineapple
4 star anise
2 pinches of saffron
2 pieces of cassia bark or
    2 cinnamon sticks
150 g (5½ oz) white (granulated)
    sugar
200 ml (7 fl oz) water

Combine the pineapple and spices in a bowl.

Meanwhile, put the sugar in a saucepan and give the pan a shake to spread it in an even layer. Place the pan over medium–low heat. Once the sugar starts to caramelise around the edges, use a spatula to bring the caramel and melted sugar to the middle of the pan. Gently stir the caramel every so often to make sure the sugar lumps dissolve. Once the caramel is completely smooth and all the sugar has caramelised, cook until it turns a dark amber. Remove the pan from the heat.

Add the pineapple mixture to the caramel. Deglaze the pan with the water and cook over medium–high heat for 15–20 minutes or until the pineapple is tender and translucent. Set aside to cool, then remove the whole spices.

ASSEMBLY

Edible flowers, to garnish
Micro mint, to garnish

Transfer the mango gel and the passionfruit curd into separate piping bags.

Spoon the coconut sago into each jar until it covers the panna cotta. Pipe a large dollop of passionfruit curd on top of the coconut sago, then add small dollops of mango gel.

Add three small spoonfuls of caramelised pineapple to each jar and garnish with edible flowers and mint.

MILLE-TUILE

My little twist on the classic mille-feuille is a little bit easier, fun, tasty and modern. Instead of spending the whole day making puff pastry, I've used tuiles. Of course, they're not as fine and flaky as puff pastry, and they do contain more sugar, so I've dialled down the sweetness by using brown sugar and reducing the amount used.

SALTED VANILLA WHIPPED GANACHE

½ gelatine sheet (titanium grade)
385 ml (13 fl oz) thickened (whipping) cream
5 g (⅛ oz) salt
Seeds of 1 vanilla bean
100 g (3 ½ oz) white chocolate

Soak the gelatine in cold water to soften.

Pour 165 ml (5½ fl oz) of the cream into a saucepan, add the salt and vanilla seeds and bring to a simmer over medium heat.

Put the white chocolate in a heatproof bowl, pour in the hot cream and stir until melted. Squeeze the excess water from the softened gelatine, add it to the cream mixture and stir until dissolved and well combined. Pass the mixture through a fine sieve, then allow it to cool to room temperature.

Stir in the remaining 220 ml (7½ fl oz) of cream. Pour the ganache into an airtight container and refrigerate overnight.

Transfer the ganache to a mixer fitted with the whisk attachment. Whisk until the mixture is very smooth and has formed medium peaks. Transfer to a piping bag fitted with a 1 cm (½ inch) round nozzle and place in the fridge until needed.

DARK BROWN SUGAR TUILE

65 g (2¼ oz) unsalted butter
115 g (4 oz) dark brown sugar
2 g (¹⁄₁₆ oz) salt
65 g (2¼ oz) plain (all-purpose) flour
85 g (3 oz) egg whites

Preheat the oven to 170°C (340°F). Line a baking sheet with a silicone mat or baking paper.

Put the butter, brown sugar and salt in a saucepan and stir over medium heat until melted and combined. Whisk in the flour, then whisk in the egg whites and mix until a smooth paste is formed. Transfer the mixture to a bowl and refrigerate for 15–20 minutes or until cool.

Spread the tuile mixture evenly over the baking sheet. Bake for 7–8 minutes or until the surface darkens slightly. Remove from the oven and set aside to cool.

Break the cooled tuile into pieces about 10 cm (4 inches) wide and 7 cm (2¾ inches) high. Working gently, trim the straightest of the long sides of each tuile to create a flat base that will help the mille-tuile stand upright. Set aside until needed or store in an airtight container. *See photograph on page 113.* →

VANILLA SALTED CARAMEL

155 g (5½ oz) liquid glucose
200 ml (7 fl oz) single (pure) cream
50 ml (1¾ fl oz) full-cream milk
5 g (⅛ oz) salt
Seeds of 1 vanilla bean
95 g (3¼ oz) white (granulated) sugar
70 g (2½ oz) unsalted butter

Combine 50 g (1¾ oz) of the glucose with the cream, milk, salt and vanilla seeds in a saucepan and bring to a simmer.

Meanwhile, combine the sugar with the remaining 105 g (3½ oz) of glucose in a saucepan and cook over medium–high heat, stirring occasionally, until the caramel turns a deep amber and reaches 182°C (360°F) on a sugar thermometer. If the caramel begins to smoke, reduce the heat to low.

Slowly whisk the hot cream mixture into the caramel and bring the mixture to the boil. Remove the pan from the heat and leave to cool until the mixture reaches 60°C (140°F), then whisk in the butter.

Strain the caramel, then transfer it to a piping bag.

ASSEMBLY

Place a tuile on a flat surface and pipe three straight lines of the whipped ganache, leaving a 5 mm (¼ inch) gap in between the lines as shown below. Pipe the caramel in the gaps between the ganache lines.

Place another tuile on top and repeat the piping and layering twice more, ensuring each layer is aligned. Repeat with the remaining tuiles. Serve immediately.

NOTE: You can do more than three layers if you like – do as many as you want!

DARK BROWN SUGAR TUILE: Trim the straightest of the long sides of each tuile to create a flat base when the tuiles stand upright.

ASSEMBLY: Pipe three lines of the whipped ganache onto one of the tuiles, then pipe the caramel in the gaps between the ganache.

THE ULTIMATE PRALINE TART

START THIS RECIPE
A DAY AHEAD

This decadent tart is based on a classic flavour trio – chocolate, caramel and peanuts. I've elevated the flavours and added a touch of coffee and hazelnuts, as well as some roasted flavours, too. With a little bit of technique and care, you can turn a simple tart into something stunning – that's what finesse is all about.

ROASTED MILK CHOCOLATE GANACHE

280 g (10 oz) milk chocolate
1 gelatine sheet (titanium grade)
140 ml (4½ fl oz) full-cream milk
200 ml (7 fl oz) thickened (whipping) cream

Preheat the oven to 150°C (300°F). Line a baking tray with baking paper and spread the chocolate on the tray. Roast for 15 minutes or until the cocoa butter has split from the chocolate and the chocolate looks dry.

Meanwhile, soak the gelatine in cold water to soften.

Pour the milk and cream into a saucepan and bring to the boil. Remove from the heat, add the roasted chocolate and use an immersion blender to blend until melted and smooth. Squeeze the excess water from the softened gelatine, add it to the pan and stir until dissolved and well combined.

Transfer the ganache to a container and refrigerate for a few hours, preferably overnight, until set.

COFFEE TART SHELL

375 g (13 oz) plain (all-purpose) flour, plus extra for dusting
80 g (2¾ oz) white (granulated) sugar
200 g (7 oz) chilled unsalted butter, cubed
10 g (¼ oz) ground coffee beans
5 g (⅛ oz) freeze-dried coffee granules
1 egg
1 egg yolk
100 g (3½ oz) dark chocolate

Preheat the oven to 170°C (340°F). Place a 20 x 2 cm (6 x ¾ inch) perforated tart ring on a baking tray lined with baking paper.

Combine the flour, sugar, butter and coffee in a mixer fitted with the paddle attachment. Mix until a sandy texture is formed. Slowly add the egg and egg yolk and mix until a dough is formed. Wrap the dough in plastic wrap and refrigerate for at least 30 minutes.

Roll out the chilled dough on a lightly floured surface to a thickness of 2 mm (¹⁄₁₆ inch). Drape the dough over the tart ring and tuck in the edges, cutting off the excess. Prick the centre of the tart shell with a skewer a few times. Line the shell with baking paper and fill with baking beads or uncooked rice. Blind bake the shell for 15 minutes. Remove the paper and beads or rice and bake for a further 15 minutes or until golden. Set aside to cool.

Melt the chocolate in a heatproof bowl in the microwave or over a saucepan of simmering water. Coat the inside of the tart shell with the melted chocolate and allow it to set. →

CRÈME PÂTISSIÈRE

500 ml (17 fl oz) full-cream milk
4 egg yolks
110 g (3¾ oz) caster (superfine) sugar
40 g (1½ oz) cornflour (cornstarch)

Pour the milk into a saucepan and bring it to a simmer.

Meanwhile, whisk the egg yolks and sugar until fluffy, then stir in the cornflour until the mixture is well combined and forms a paste-like consistency.

Whisk the hot milk into the egg yolk mixture, then pour the mixture back into the pan and whisk over medium heat until it has thickened to a very firm custard-like consistency. Immediately use the hot crème pâtissière to make the peanut butter diplomat cream (see below).

PEANUT BUTTER DIPLOMAT CREAM

1 gelatine sheet (titanium grade)
1 quantity crème pâtissière
    (see above)
175 g (6 oz) smooth peanut butter
250 ml (9 fl oz) thickened (whipping) cream

Soak the gelatine in cold water to soften.

Pour the hot crème pâtissière into a jug. Squeeze the excess water from the softened gelatine and add it to the jug, along with the peanut butter. Using an immersion blender, blend until the mixture is completely smooth. Transfer the mixture to a bowl and refrigerate for 30–45 minutes or until cool.

Whisk the cream until medium peaks form, then fold it through the crème pâtissière mixture. Place in the fridge until needed.

PEANUT & HAZELNUT PRALINE PASTE

150 g (5½ oz) unsalted peanuts
150 g (5½ oz) blanched hazelnuts
200 g (7 oz) caster (superfine) sugar

Preheat the oven to 170°C (340°F). Line a large baking tray with baking paper. Spread the peanuts and hazelnuts over another baking tray and roast for 10–15 minutes or until golden.

Meanwhile, put the sugar in a saucepan and give the pan a shake to spread it in an even layer. Place the pan over medium–low heat. Once the sugar starts to caramelise around the edges, use a spatula to bring the caramel and melted sugar to the middle of the pan. Gently stir the caramel every so often to make sure the sugar lumps dissolve. Once the caramel is completely smooth and all the sugar has caramelised, cook until it turns a dark amber. Remove the pan from the heat.

Stir the nuts into the caramel, then pour the mixture onto the lined tray and set aside until completely cooled.

Break the nut mixture into small pieces and place it in a high-speed blender. Blend until the mixture forms a wet, oily paste – it should take about 4–5 minutes. Once the mixture is smooth, transfer it to an airtight container and store at room temperature until needed. →

ASSEMBLY

Dark cocoa powder, for dusting
Roasted hazelnuts, to garnish
Roasted peanut halves, to garnish

Use the back of a spoon to spread the peanut and hazelnut praline paste in the tart shell in a 5 mm (¼ inch) thick layer (see below). Place in the fridge to set for 10 minutes.

Transfer the peanut butter diplomat cream to a piping bag. Pipe a 1 cm (½ inch) layer of the diplomat cream on top of the praline, leaving a 5 mm (¼ inch) gap from the top of the tart shell.

Transfer the roasted milk chocolate ganache to a piping bag fitted with a large petal piping tip (no. 104). Starting at the edge of the tart, pipe the ganache in a random left-to-right motion without stopping until the top of the tart is covered, as shown. Place the tart in the fridge for 10–15 minutes or until ready to serve.

Lightly dust the tart with cocoa powder just before serving and garnish with the hazelnuts and peanuts.

ASSEMBLY: Spread the peanut and hazelnut praline paste over the chocolate-coated tart shell.

Pipe the roasted milk chocolate ganache in a constant left-to-right motion until it covers the top of the tart.

OPERA

The classic French opera is a layered almond sponge cake, flavoured with coffee and chocolate and made with layers of buttercream and chocolate ganache. I have added jasmine tea to the ganache, bringing a floral note to the rich chocolate and espresso that lingers throughout the cake. This is not your typical opera cake ... it's even better.

The gold rings adorning the top of the cake are optional, but I think they add an extra sense of luxury.

SABLÉ BASE

250 g (9 oz) unsalted butter, softened
375 g (13 oz) almond meal
315 g (11 oz) caster (superfine) sugar
125 g (4½ oz) plain (all-purpose) flour
5 g (⅛ oz) salt
100 g (3½ oz) cocoa butter

Preheat the oven to 170°C (340°F). Line two baking trays with baking paper and place a 20 cm (8 inch) square stainless steel pastry frame on one of the trays.

Combine the butter, almond meal, sugar, flour and salt in a mixer fitted with the paddle attachment. Mix until a dough is formed.

Evenly spread the dough over the baking tray and bake for 15–20 minutes or until golden brown. Allow to cool, then transfer the sablé to a food processor and process until crumbs are formed. Transfer the crumbs to a bowl.

Melt the cocoa butter in a heatproof bowl in the microwave or over a saucepan of simmering water, then add it to the sablé crumbs and mix until combined. Spread the crumb mix inside the pastry frame and press it down with an offset palette knife to make it completely level. Place the base in the fridge to set. →

JASMINE CHOCOLATE GANACHE

215 g (7½ oz) 55% dark chocolate
250 ml (9 fl oz) single (pure) cream
10 g (¼ oz) jasmine tea leaves

Melt the chocolate in a heatproof bowl in the microwave or over a saucepan of simmering water.

Meanwhile, combine the cream and tea in a small saucepan and bring to the boil over medium heat. When the cream has come to the boil, remove from the heat and allow it to infuse for 5 minutes.

Using a fine sieve, strain the cream onto the chocolate and stir until combined. Use an immersion blender to blend the ganache for 1–2 minutes or until it is completely smooth.

Pour the ganache onto the sablé base. Gently tap the tray to level the ganache, then set it aside while you prepare the joconde.

JOCONDE

10 eggs, separated
60 g (2¼ oz) unsalted butter, melted
90 g (3¼ oz) plain (all-purpose) flour
300 g (10½ oz) almond meal
250 g (9 oz) icing (confectioners')
    sugar

Preheat the oven to 170°C (340°F). Line two baking trays with baking paper.

Put the egg yolks in a mixer fitted with the whisk attachment and whisk on high speed until the yolks are pale in colour and have doubled in size. Reduce the speed to low and slowly pour in the melted butter, whisking until just combined. Transfer the mixture to a bowl and set aside.

Place the egg whites in the cleaned mixer bowl and whisk on high speed until stiff peaks form.

Meanwhile, sift the flour, almond meal and icing sugar into a large bowl. Fold in the egg yolk mixture in two batches, then fold in the meringue.

Divide the batter between the baking trays and use a palette knife to spread it evenly over the trays. Bake for 14 minutes or until the sponges bounce back to the touch. Allow to cool, then trim each joconde to a 20 cm (8 inch) square. Place one joconde square on top of the jasmine ganache. Reserve the second joconde square.

COFFEE BUTTERCREAM

15 g (½ oz) freeze-dried coffee
    granules
35 ml (1 fl oz) water
70 ml (2¼ fl oz) full-cream milk
60 g (2¼ oz) egg yolks
160 g (5½ oz) caster (superfine) sugar
335 g (11¾ oz) softened unsalted
    butter, cubed
45 g (1½ oz) egg whites

Combine the coffee granules and the water and stir to dissolve the coffee.

Pour the milk into a small saucepan and bring to the boil over medium heat.

Meanwhile, put the egg yolks and 70 g (2½ oz) of the sugar in a small bowl and whisk until well combined. Pour in a little of the boiling milk and whisk well. Pour the mixture into the pan with the remaining milk and stir the anglaise until it reaches 85°C (185°F) on a sugar thermometer. Add the coffee mixture.

Pour the cooled anglaise into a mixer fitted with the whisk attachment and whisk on high speed until it reaches 50°C (122°F). Add the butter, a cube at a time, whisking well before adding the next piece. Transfer the buttercream mixture to a bowl and set aside.

Put the egg whites in the cleaned mixer bowl and whisk with the remaining 90 g (3¼ oz) of sugar until stiff peaks form.

Fold the meringue into the buttercream, then spread it evenly over the joconde in the pastry frame. Carefully place the reserved joconde square on top of the buttercream. Place in the freezer while you prepare the coffee mousse. →

COFFEE MOUSSE

1 gelatine sheet (titanium grade)
100 ml single (pure) cream
1 egg yolk
10 g (¼ oz) caster (superfine) sugar
10 g (¼ oz) freeze-dried coffee
  granules
50 g (1¾ oz) white chocolate
125 ml (4 fl oz) thickened (whipping)
  cream

Soak the gelatine in cold water to soften.

Pour the single cream into a small saucepan. Bring to the boil over medium heat.

Meanwhile, whisk the egg yolk and sugar in a heatproof bowl until fluffy. Whisk in the hot cream, then pour the mixture back into the pan and cook, stirring constantly, until the anglaise thickens and reaches 85°C (185°F) on a sugar thermometer. Remove the pan from the heat. Squeeze the excess water from the softened gelatine, add it to the anglaise with the coffee and whisk until dissolved and well combined.

Put the white chocolate in a bowl and, using a fine sieve, strain the anglaise onto the chocolate. Whisk until smooth, then leave the mixture to cool to 40°C (104°F).

Meanwhile, whip the thickened cream until medium peaks form. Fold the cream through the coffee mixture. Pour the mousse over the joconde and use an offset palette knife to level it. Place the cake in the freezer, making sure it is level, for 30 minutes or until frozen.

DARK CHOCOLATE GLAZE

145 ml (4¾ fl oz) water
180 g (6 oz) caster (superfine) sugar
90 g (3¼ oz) liquid glucose
120 ml (3¾ fl oz) single (pure) cream
3 gelatine sheets (titanium grade)
60 g (2¼ oz) dark cocoa powder

Put the water, sugar, glucose and cream in a saucepan and stir to combine. Bring to the boil over medium heat, then remove from the heat and cool until the mixture reaches 65°C (149°F) on a sugar thermometer.

Meanwhile, soak the gelatine in cold water to soften.

Add the cocoa to the cream mixture and stir until completely combined and smooth. Allow the mixture to cool to 45°C (113°F). Squeeze the excess water from the softened gelatine, add it to the chocolate mixture and stir until dissolved and well combined. Use an immersion blender to blend the glaze until it is completely smooth and any air bubbles have been removed, then strain it into a jug. Pour the glaze over the mousse to form the final layer and refrigerate until set.

ASSEMBLY

50 ml (1¾ fl oz) vodka
1 teaspoon edible gold dust

Gently warm the outside of the pastry frame with a blowtorch to help release it. Warm a long sharp knife in hot water, then wipe the knife and slice the cake in half to make two 10 x 20 cm (4 x 8 inch) slabs. Using a ruler as a guide, cut each slab into 4 x 10 cm (1½ x 4 inch) slices, heating and wiping the knife blade before each cut.

Put the vodka and gold dust in a small bowl and stir to combine.

Use a 2 cm (¾ inch) round cutter and a 4 cm (1½ inch) round cutter to decorate the chocolate glaze by dipping the edges of the cutters into the vodka and then carefully pressing them onto the glaze to make gold rings. Serve immediately or return to the fridge until serving.

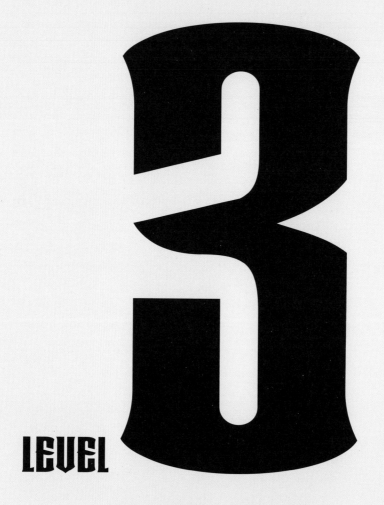

LEVEL

FOR THE
SERIOUS COOKS

Are (You) an adventure baker?

Level 3

HERE IS A COLLECTION OF RECIPES THAT WOULD BE DIFFICULT EVEN FOR MY CHEFS, INCLUDING A FEW THAT ARE MY SIGNATURE DISHES.

1

You'll find components of recipes from the previous chapters that have been repeated or slightly *tweaked*. Not everything has to be unique — it's all about *redesigning recipes* and imagining how the dish will be constructed. In the end it's like a form of art, design or fashion, considering everything from the way it looks to the way it tastes and the way you eat it, with each ingredient and element determining the outcome.

2

Creativity is the fuel for my craft — it's literally the make or break for my life and career. I get bored easily and I have an itch to constantly keep creating, otherwise what's the point of cooking? Where's the *flair?* Where's the *passion?* When I'm creating a dish I like to work around a theme, which allows me to work with a structure and some form of guidance. Just like an artist working with colours, whether using a singular colour or a spectrum, I focus on imagining what the dish will look like, the story, the temperature, texture and taste.

3

These recipes aren't all that difficult, they just look complex because of the design and thought process behind them. Use the recipes to replicate my dishes, or use them as a foundation for an even greater dish. Let your *imagination run wild* and build dishes with flavour charting (see pages 10–13), exploring how ingredients can be transformed when treated in different ways. Overall, *have fun* — always let that be the key focus, and enjoy the process, because anyone can cook!

NOMTELLA

START THIS RECIPE
A DAY AHEAD

Nomtella is one of our three signatures at KOI and one of my first creations for the dessert bar. It started out as a plated dessert at a pop-up event back in 2015, but it felt so empty. I redesigned it into a cake and it's now one of our bestsellers. I love the classic combination of coffee, hazelnut, chocolate and caramel – dark, roasted, nutty and caramelised flavours. The real winner of this dessert is the texture and how sexy it looks with the chocolate glaze and a splash of gold.

SALTED CARAMEL INSERTS

155 g (5½ oz) liquid glucose
200 ml (7 fl oz) single (pure) cream
50 ml (1¾ fl oz) full-cream milk
5 g (⅛ oz) salt
Seeds of 1 vanilla bean
95 g (3¼ oz) white (granulated) sugar
70 g (2½ oz) unsalted butter, cubed

Combine 50 g (1¾ oz) of the glucose with the cream, milk, salt and vanilla seeds in a saucepan and bring to a simmer.

Meanwhile, combine the sugar with the remaining 105 g (3½ oz) of glucose in another saucepan. Cook over medium–high heat, stirring occasionally, until the mixture turns a deep-brown amber and reaches a temperature of 182°C (360°F) on a sugar thermometer.

Slowly whisk in the butter until emulsified, then pour in the hot cream mixture and bring to the boil. Cook for 15–20 minutes or until the caramel is thick and reduced by a third (don't overcook or it may split). Set aside until completely cool. If the caramel isn't firm like a ganache, return it to the heat to reduce further.

Transfer the caramel to a piping bag. Pipe eight 3 cm (1¼ inch) rounds onto a tray lined with baking paper and freeze until solid.

ESPRESSO MOUSSE

2 gelatine sheets (titanium grade)
135 ml (4½ fl oz) full-cream milk
20 g (¾ oz) freeze-dried coffee
   granules
45 g (1½ oz) egg yolks
30 g (1 oz) white (granulated) sugar
280 g (10 oz) white chocolate
Ice cubes
630 ml (21½ fl oz) thickened
   (whipping) cream
8 salted caramel inserts (see above)

Soak the gelatine in cold water to soften.

Combine the milk and coffee in a small saucepan and bring to a simmer.

Meanwhile, whisk the egg yolks and sugar in a small heatproof bowl until fluffy. Slowly whisk in the hot milk mixture. Pour the mixture back into the pan and cook, whisking constantly, until the anglaise reaches 84°C (183°F) on a sugar thermometer. Remove from the heat. Squeeze the excess water from the softened gelatine, add it to the anglaise and whisk until dissolved and well combined.

Add the white chocolate and stir until melted. Pass the anglaise through a fine sieve into a large metal bowl sitting in an ice bath. Leave to cool to below 25°C (77°F).

Whip the cream until medium peaks form. Fold the cream into the cooled anglaise mixture in three batches. Transfer the mousse to a piping bag and pipe it into eight 6.5 cm (2½ inch) silicone stone moulds, filling them almost to the top.

Press a salted caramel insert into each mould, then add enough mousse to cover the insert and fill the mould. Level the surface, then freeze overnight.

See photographs on page 132. ➔

ESPRESSO MOUSSE: Pipe the mousse into silicone stone moulds, filling them almost to the top.

Press one of the frozen salted caramel inserts down into the mousse in each mould.

Add enough of the mousse to cover the salted caramel inserts, then level the surface of each mould.

ASSEMBLY: Pour the chocolate glaze over the frozen mousse rounds until they are evenly coated.

BROWNIE BASE

Oil spray, for greasing
270 g (9½ oz) 60% dark chocolate
250 g (9 oz) unsalted butter
4 eggs
240 g (8½ oz) white (granulated)
　sugar
80 g (2¾ oz) dark cocoa powder
60 g (2¼ oz) plain (all-purpose) flour
1 teaspoon baking powder

Preheat the oven to 170°C (340°F). Line a shallow baking tray with baking paper and spray with oil.

Combine the chocolate and butter in a heatproof bowl over a saucepan of simmering water and stir occasionally until melted. Remove from the heat and fold in the eggs.

Sift the sugar, cocoa, flour and baking powder onto the chocolate mixture and fold until a batter is formed.

Spoon the brownie batter onto the baking tray and spread until it is 1.5 cm (⅝ inch) thick. Bake the brownie for 15–22 minutes or until the centre is cooked and not too wet. Cool slightly, then place the brownie in the freezer to cool.

Using a 5 cm (2 inch) round cutter, cut eight rounds from the brownie. Place in an airtight container in the fridge or freezer until needed.

CHOCOLATE GLAZE

6 gelatine sheets (titanium grade)
290 ml (10 fl oz) water
240 ml (8 fl oz) thickened (whipping)
　cream
360 g (12¾ oz) white (granulated)
　sugar
120 g (4¼ oz) dark cocoa powder
75 g (2½ oz) liquid glucose

Soak the gelatine in cold water to soften.

Combine the water, cream, sugar, cocoa and glucose in a saucepan. Whisk over medium heat until simmering, then remove from the heat. Squeeze the excess water from the softened gelatine, add it to the pan and whisk until dissolved and well combined.

Using an immersion blender, blend the mixture until glossy. Strain the glaze into a jug and set aside to cool to 28°C (82°F).

ASSEMBLY

16 roasted hazelnuts
Fennel fronds, to garnish
Edible gold dust, to garnish

Unmould the frozen mousse rounds and place them on a wire rack with a tray underneath to catch the excess chocolate glaze.

Check the temperature of the chocolate glaze. If needed, gently reheat it in the microwave until it is between 28°C (82°F) and 30°C (86°F).

Pour the glaze over one of the mousse rounds until evenly coated (see left). Using a small spatula, release the glazed mousse from the wire rack and place it on top of one of the brownie circles. Repeat with the remaining mousse rounds. Place each cake on a serving plate.

Halve eight of the hazelnuts, then roughly chop eight of the hazelnut halves. Garnish each cake with a whole hazelnut, a hazelnut half and some chopped hazelnuts. Finish with a sprig of fennel and gold dust.

BALI SUNRISE

This name triggers my memory of the restaurant my parents owned in Australia a long time ago. I decided to name this dessert after the restaurant, as growing up I loved the dessert drink Mum and Dad used to serve called *cendol* (chen-doll). It's a starch pandan jelly served with coconut milk and palm sugar, sometimes with pieces of jackfruit, too. You'd find this drink being sold by street vendors and in almost every restaurant in Indonesia.

COCONUT JACKFRUIT MOUSSE

1 gelatine sheet (titanium grade)
250 g (9 oz) coconut cream
40 g (1½ oz) white (granulated) sugar
2 g (1/16 oz) salt
100 ml (3½ fl oz) thickened (whipping) cream
50 g (1¾ oz) jackfruit, cut into small cubes

Soak the gelatine in cold water to soften.

Combine the coconut cream, sugar and salt in a saucepan and bring to a simmer. Squeeze the excess water from the softened gelatine, add it to the pan and whisk until dissolved and well combined. Transfer the coconut mixture to a bowl and place in the fridge for about 30 minutes or until semi-set.

Whisk the cream until medium peaks form. Whisk in the semi-set coconut mixture and the jackfruit until combined.

Transfer the mousse to a piping bag and pipe it into eight 5 cm (2 inch) diameter silicone hemisphere moulds. Place in the fridge for 30 minutes or until set.

Use a 2 cm (¾ inch) melon baller to scoop out and discard (or eat!) the centre of each mousse half. Transfer the mousse halves to the freezer while you prepare the pandan gel.

PANDAN GEL

200 ml (7 fl oz) water
80 g (2¾ oz) white (granulated) sugar
4 g (⅛ oz) pandan extract
3 g (⅛ oz) agar

Combine the water, sugar, pandan extract and agar in a saucepan and whisk over high heat until boiling. Pour the mixture into a container and place in the fridge for 30 minutes or until the jelly is completely set.

Cut the jelly into rough cubes and place them in a blender. Blend on high speed until completely smooth, then strain the gel into a squeeze bottle.

Pipe the pandan gel into the centre of each frozen coconut mousse half, filling them almost to the top. Return the mousse halves to the freezer and freeze overnight or until solid.

Remove the mousse halves from the moulds. Lightly warm the flat surfaces of the frozen mousse halves on a warm tray and join the halves together to form four spheres. Store the mousse spheres in the freezer until needed. →

CHOCOLATE DIP

150 g (5½ oz) dark chocolate
150 g (5½ oz) cocoa butter

Combine the chocolate and cocoa butter in a heatproof bowl over a saucepan of simmering water and stir occasionally until melted. Transfer the chocolate dip to a 500 ml (17 fl oz) measuring jug.

Insert a bamboo skewer in the base of one of the frozen coconut mousse spheres as shown below and submerge it into the chocolate dip. Using a pastry brush, quickly brush all over the chocolate as it's setting in up and down strokes, until the sphere resembles a coconut. Remove the skewer and seal the pierced hole with a drop of chocolate dip. Place on a tray and repeat with the remaining mousse spheres.

Lightly heat a melon baller and use it to create three dimples on the top of each coconut as shown. Place the coconuts in the fridge to thaw for at least an hour before serving. ➜

CHOCOLATE DIP: Insert a skewer into the base of one of the frozen mousse spheres before submerging it into the chocolate dip.

Use a heated melon baller to create three dimples on the top of each mousse sphere to resemble a coconut.

PALM SUGAR SAND

100 g (3½ oz) palm sugar (jaggery)
100 g (3½ oz) unsalted butter
100 g (3½ oz) almond meal
55 g (2 oz) plain (all-purpose) flour
2 pinches of salt
50 g (1¾ oz) white chocolate
15 g (½ oz) maltodextrin

Preheat the oven to 170°C (340°F). Line a baking tray with baking paper.

Combine the palm sugar, butter, almond meal, flour and salt in a mixer fitted with the paddle attachment. Mix until a dough is formed.

Transfer the dough onto the baking tray and roll out until it is 1 cm (½ inch) thick. Bake for 15–17 minutes or until golden brown. Allow to cool completely.

Reduce the oven to 160°C (320°F). Line a baking tray with baking paper. Spread the white chocolate on the tray and roast for 15–17 minutes or until the chocolate is golden and the cocoa butter has split from the chocolate.

Break the cooked dough into pieces and transfer to a food processor. Lightly blend, then add the roasted white chocolate and maltodextrin and briefly pulse until crumbly. (Don't overblend the mixture or it will turn into a paste.)

Store the palm sugar sand in a container in the fridge.

PASSIONFRUIT & PINEAPPLE JELLY

150 ml (5 fl oz) passionfruit juice
150 ml (5 fl oz) pineapple juice
35 ml (1 fl oz) lime juice
20 g (¾ oz) caster (superfine) sugar
4 g (⅛ oz) agar

Combine the passionfruit juice, pineapple juice, lime juice, sugar and agar in a saucepan and whisk over medium heat until boiling. Pour the mixture into a container and refrigerate for 30 minutes or until the jelly is completely set.

Cut the jelly into 5 mm (¼ inch) cubes and store in the fridge until needed.

ASSEMBLY

100 g (3½ oz) pineapple, finely diced
1 passionfruit
Micro mint, to garnish
Edible flowers, to garnish (optional)

Place 1 tablespoon of the palm sugar sand on four serving plates and create a well in the centre of each. Place a coconut on top of the sand on each plate, with the three dimples facing up.

Arrange spoonfuls of the passionfruit and pineapple jelly beside the coconuts and top with the diced pineapple, passionfruit pulp, mint leaves and flowers, if using.

MOSS

This signature dessert has been on the menu at KOI since day one, but it has evolved year after year. It was the first monochrome-inspired dessert. Because it was based on the colour green, I wanted it to have earthy notes. It was an unusual flavour combination, but somehow everything sang harmoniously and it entranced our diners, who came back for more, again and again.

PISTACHIO MONTE

½ gelatine sheet (titanium grade)
45 g (1½ oz) white chocolate
25 g (1 oz) pistachio paste (see Note)
180 ml (5½ fl oz) thickened
  (whipping) cream
15 g (½ oz) white (granulated) sugar

Soak the gelatine in cold water to soften.

Meanwhile, combine the white chocolate and pistachio paste in a heatproof bowl over a saucepan of simmering water and stir occasionally until melted. Squeeze the excess water from the softened gelatine, add it to the pistachio mixture and stir until dissolved and well combined.

Combine the cream and sugar in a mixer fitted with the whisk attachment and whisk until medium peaks form. Slowly fold the cream into the pistachio mixture.

Pour the pistachio mousse into twelve 5 cm (2 inch) diameter silicone hemisphere moulds. Place in the fridge for 30 minutes to set.

Use a 2 cm (¾ inch) melon baller to scoop out and discard (or eat!) the centre of each mousse half. Transfer the mousse halves to the freezer while you prepare the caramel gel.

NOTE: You'll find pistachio paste in specialty food stores. Alternatively, you can use a chocolate hazelnut spread (such as Nutella).

CARAMEL GEL

100 g (3½ oz) white (granulated)
  sugar
140 ml (4½ fl oz) boiling water
1.8 g (¹⁄₁₆ oz) agar (approximately)
Salt
20 ml (¾ fl oz) single (pure) cream

Put the sugar in a saucepan and give the pan a shake to spread it in an even layer. Place the pan over medium–low heat. Once the sugar starts to caramelise around the edges, use a spatula to bring the caramel and melted sugar to the middle of the pan. Gently stir the caramel every so often to make sure the sugar lumps dissolve. Once the caramel is completely smooth and all the sugar has caramelised, cook until it turns a dark amber.

Remove the pan from the heat and carefully whisk in the boiling water, a little at a time. Return the pan to the heat and whisk until all the caramel has dissolved again. Transfer the caramel mixture to a jug. Weigh the liquid and add 0.75% of the weight in agar. For example, 200 g (7 oz) of liquid would need 1.5 g (¹⁄₁₆ oz) of agar.

Return the mixture to the pan and whisk vigorously. Bring to the boil over medium heat, boil for 10 seconds and then remove from the heat. Pour the mixture into a container and place in the fridge for 15–20 minutes or until set. →

Cut the jelly into rough cubes and place them in a blender. Blend the jelly on high speed until smooth, then season with salt and a dash of cream and blend again. Transfer the gel to a squeeze bottle.

Pipe the caramel gel into the centre of each frozen pistachio mousse half, filling them almost to the top. Return the mousse to the freezer and freeze overnight or until solid.

PISTACHIO SPONGE

50 g (1¾ oz) pistachio paste
6 eggs
3 egg whites
120 g (4¼ oz) white (granulated) sugar
30 g (1 oz) plain (all-purpose) flour

Use a skewer to poke five holes in the base of four microwave-safe takeaway coffee cups.

Put all of the sponge ingredients in a jug and blend with an immersion blender until combined.

Strain the mixture into a cream whipper and charge twice with N2O as shown below. Siphon the mixture into the cups until half full. Microwave each sponge on high for 45 seconds or until the top is dry to the touch. Allow the sponges to cool upside down on a wire rack before removing from the cups.

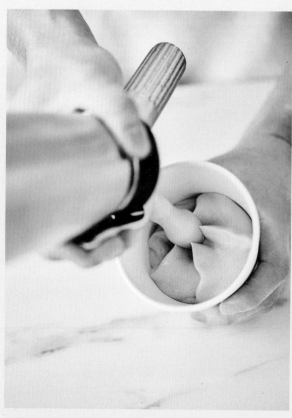

PISTACHIO SPONGE: Strain the blended sponge mixture into a cream whipper and siphon it into the cups until they are half full.

Microwave the sponges until the tops are dry to the touch, then leave them to cool before removing them from the cups.

CRÈME PÂTISSIÈRE

250 ml (9 fl oz) full-cream milk
2 egg yolks
55 g (2 oz) white (granulated) sugar
20 g (¾ oz) cornflour (cornstarch)

Pour the milk into a saucepan and bring it to a simmer.

Meanwhile, whisk the egg yolks and sugar until fluffy, then stir in the cornflour until the mixture is well combined and forms a paste-like consistency.

Whisk the hot milk into the egg yolk mixture, then pour the mixture back into the pan and whisk over medium heat until it has thickened to a very firm custard-like consistency. Immediately use the hot crème pâtissière to make the dulce crémeux (see below).

DULCE CRÉMEUX

½ gelatine sheet (titanium grade)
90 g (3¼ oz) white chocolate
1 quantity crème pâtissière
   (see above)
125 ml (4 fl oz) thickened (whipping)
   cream

Preheat the oven to 160°C (320°F). Line a baking tray with baking paper.

Soak the gelatine in cold water to soften.

Meanwhile, spread the white chocolate on the baking tray and roast for 15–17 minutes or until the chocolate is golden and the cocoa butter has split from the chocolate.

Pour the hot crème pâtissière into a jug. Squeeze the excess water from the softened gelatine and add it to the jug, along with the roasted chocolate. Using an immersion blender, blend until the mixture is completely smooth. Transfer the mixture to a bowl and refrigerate for 4–5 hours or until cooled.

Whisk the cream until medium peaks form, then slowly fold it through the crème pâtissière. Transfer the mixture to a piping bag and place in the fridge.

MATCHA SOIL

150 g (5½ oz) white (granulated)
   sugar
80 g (2¾ oz) plain (all-purpose) flour
65 g (2¼ oz) almond meal
50 g (1¾ oz) rice flour
25 g (1 oz) matcha powder
80 g (2¾ oz) butter
1 egg

Preheat the oven to 150°C (300°F). Line a baking tray with baking paper.

Combine the sugar, flour, almond meal, rice flour, matcha powder and butter in a mixer fitted with the paddle attachment. Mix on low speed until a sandy texture is formed, then add the egg and mix until a dough is formed.

Break the dough into rough chunks, about 5 cm (2 inches) each, and place on the baking tray. Bake for 18 minutes or until slightly browned on the edges. Allow to cool completely, then transfer the cooked dough to a food processor and blitz until crumbly. Store in an airtight container. ➜

MATCHA DIP

300 g (10½ oz) white chocolate
150 g (5½ oz) cocoa butter
15 g (½ oz) matcha powder

Combine the white chocolate, cocoa butter and matcha powder in a heatproof bowl over a saucepan of simmering water and stir occasionally until melted. Transfer the matcha dip to a 500 ml (17 fl oz) measuring jug and set aside to cool to 40°C (104°F).

Remove the frozen pistachio mousse halves from the moulds. Lightly warm the flat surfaces of the frozen mousse halves on a warm tray. Working quickly, join the halves together to make four mousse spheres, removing as much of the seams as possible. While still frozen, skewer the base of each mousse sphere with a bamboo skewer and immediately lower it into the matcha dip until completely submerged. Allow the excess dip to drip off, then remove the skewer and seal the hole with a warm knife. Repeat with the remaining spheres. Place the spheres in the fridge to thaw for a few hours.

ASSEMBLY

1 green apple, thinly sliced
Matcha powder, for dusting
Micro mint, to garnish
Fennel fronds, to garnish
Buckler sorrel, to garnish (optional)

Pipe a dollop of the dulce crémeux in the centre of six serving plates, then top with a generous spoonful of matcha soil. Place the dipped pistachio mousse spheres on top of the dulce crémeux and then pipe four more dollops of dulce crémeux around each sphere.

Rip the pistachio sponge cakes into pieces and place them around the spheres.

Place thin slices of green apple in between the sponge cake and the spheres, then dust with matcha powder and garnish with sprigs of mint, fennel fronds and sorrel leaves, if using. Serve immediately.

AN APPLE A DAY

START THIS RECIPE
A DAY AHEAD

I wanted to create a dish to showcase every part of an apple – from the juice, to the flesh and even the tree itself. It's almost like the circle of life of an apple.

APPLEWOOD CRÈME PÂTISSIÈRE

15 g (½ oz) applewood chips
350 ml (12 fl oz) full-cream milk
2 egg yolks
55 g (2 oz) white (granulated) sugar
20 g (¾ oz) cornflour (cornstarch)

Preheat the oven to 160°C (320°F). Spread the applewood chips on a baking tray and bake for 15 minutes.

Pour the milk into a saucepan and bring to a simmer over low heat. Whisk in the applewood chips, then pour the mixture into a container and refrigerate overnight.

Strain the milk through a fine sieve into a measuring jug. Pour 250 ml (9 fl oz) of the milk into a saucepan and bring to a simmer.

Meanwhile, whisk the egg yolks and sugar until fluffy, then stir in the cornflour until the mixture is well combined and forms a paste-like consistency.

Whisk the hot milk into the egg yolk mixture, then pour the mixture back into the pan and whisk over medium heat until it has thickened to a very firm custard-like consistency. Immediately use the hot crème pâtissière to make the applewood diplomat cream (see below).

APPLEWOOD DIPLOMAT CREAM

½ gelatine sheet (titanium grade)
90 g (3¼ oz) white chocolate
1 quantity applewood crème pâtissière (see above)
125 ml (4 fl oz) thickened (whipping) cream

Soak the gelatine in cold water to soften.

Put the white chocolate in a jug and add the hot crème pâtissière. Squeeze the excess water from the softened gelatine and add it to the jug. Using an immersion blender, blend until the mixture is completely smooth. Transfer the mixture to a bowl and refrigerate for 30–45 minutes or until cool.

Whisk the cream until medium peaks form, then fold it through the crème pâtissière mixture. Place in the fridge until needed.

APPLE SHELLS

500 ml (17 fl oz) chilled water
150 ml (5 fl oz) lemon juice
4 green apples with stems

Combine the water and lemon juice in a bowl. Slice off the apple tops, cutting low enough to ensure the stems don't fall off. Add the apple tops to the lemon water.

Using a melon baller, carefully hollow out the inside of each apple, leaving a 5 mm (¼ inch) thick shell. Reserve the apple flesh for the apple caramel (see page 149). Add the apple shells to the lemon water to soak for 5–7 minutes.

Drain the apple tops and shells and pat dry with paper towel. Place in a container and store in the freezer until needed. ➜

APPLE COMPOTE

2 green apples
15 g (½ oz) unsalted butter
80 g (2¾ oz) caster (superfine) sugar
20 ml (½ fl oz) yuzu juice
15 ml (½ fl oz) whisky
Seeds of ½ vanilla bean

Peel and roughly dice the apples into 1 cm (½ inch) cubes.

Melt the butter in a small saucepan over medium heat, then add the sugar and cook until the sugar begins to colour. Add the apple, yuzu juice, whisky and vanilla seeds and cook for 25 minutes or until the apple has softened. Transfer to a container and place in the fridge to cool.

APPLE ICE FLOWERS

55 ml (1¾ fl oz) water
35 g (1¼ oz) liquid glucose
55 g (2 oz) caster (superfine) sugar
2 green apples, roughly chopped
500 g (1 lb 2 oz) green apple purée
Juice of ½ lemon

Combine the water, glucose and sugar in a saucepan over medium heat. Bring to a simmer, then remove the syrup from the heat.

Put the chopped apple, apple purée, lemon juice and syrup in a blender. Blend on high for 2–3 minutes or until smooth. Pass the mixture through a fine mesh sieve lined with cheesecloth, squeezing out as much liquid as possible.

Pour the apple liquid into flower-shaped silicone moulds and freeze until solid.

APPLE CARAMEL

Excess apple flesh (see apple shells, page 146)
2 pinches of citric acid
50 ml (1¾ fl oz) water

Juice the apple flesh in a cold-press juicer. Pour the juice into a saucepan and add the citric acid. Cook over low heat until the liquid begins to caramelise and thicken.

Slowly whisk in the water (be careful as it will spit and steam up). Bring to the boil, then remove from the heat. The caramel should have a thick, honey-like consistency.

ASSEMBLY

Fennel fronds, to garnish
Edible flowers, to garnish
Crushed ice, to serve

Transfer the applewood diplomat cream to a piping bag and pipe it into the frozen apple shells, filling them halfway. Use the back of a wet spoon to create a well in the cream. Fill the well with the apple compote.

Drizzle a teaspoon of apple caramel over the apple compote, then place an apple ice flower on top (it should sit just below the edge of the apple shell). Use the fennel and flowers to fill in the gaps. Replace the apple tops to cover the filling and place on a bed of ice. Serve immediately.

PEAR & YUZU

A dessert that looks just like the fruit it's made from seems to be the 'old age new'. It was trendy back when Heston Blumenthal did it and also when Cedric Grolet brought his signature style of incredibly stunning fruit desserts. Here's my take on a fruit-shaped pear dessert that's fresh, light and fragrant, and fun to create.

It's simplest to make it with a pear-shaped mould but you can shape it by hand, although it does take more time and effort.

STEWED PEAR INSERTS

1 beurre bosc pear
Juice of ½ lemon
20 g (¾ oz) butter
60 g (2¼ oz) white (granulated) sugar
1 teaspoon vanilla extract
1 teaspoon ground ginger
1 teaspoon pectin NH powder

Peel and dice the pear into 5 mm (¼ inch) cubes. Toss the pear with the lemon juice.

Melt the butter in a saucepan over medium heat and stir in the pear. Combine the sugar, vanilla, ginger and pectin, then add the mixture to the pan and stir well. Cook for 15–20 minutes or until the pear has softened.

Spoon the pear mixture into four 2.5 cm (1 inch) diameter silicone sphere moulds and freeze until solid.

PEAR & YUZU WHIPPED GANACHE

½ gelatine sheet (titanium grade)
165 ml (5½ fl oz) thickened (whipping) cream
Seeds of 1 vanilla bean
45 g (1½ oz) white chocolate
50 g (1¾ oz) pear purée
10 ml (¼ fl oz) yuzu juice

Soak the gelatine in cold water to soften.

Combine half of the cream in a saucepan with the vanilla seeds and bring to a simmer. Remove the pan from the heat. Squeeze the excess water from the softened gelatine, add it to the pan and stir until dissolved and well combined.

Put the white chocolate in a bowl, pour in the hot cream mixture and stir until melted and well combined. Stir in the pear purée and yuzu juice, then pour in the remaining cream and mix until well combined. Refrigerate for 1–2 hours or until set.

Transfer the pear mixture to a mixer fitted with the whisk attachment and whisk until stiff peaks form. Transfer the whipped ganache to a piping bag. Pipe the whipped ganache into four pear-shaped silicone moulds, leaving a 2 cm (¾ inch) gap at the top. Press a frozen stewed pear insert down into each pear cavity. Cover with more ganache, then level the surface with a spatula. Place the pears in the freezer. Reserve the left-over ganache for assembly. *See photograph on page 152.*

CHOCOLATE TWIGS

50 g (1¾ oz) dark chocolate
Ice

Melt the chocolate in a heatproof bowl in the microwave or over a saucepan of simmering water. Transfer to a piping bag and cut 1 cm (½ inch) off the tip.

Pipe the chocolate into a bowl of iced water to create twigs. Once set, remove the twigs from the water and drain on paper towel. Store in the fridge until needed. →

COCOA BUTTER COATING

150 g (5½ oz) cocoa butter
Green apple colouring (fat soluble)
Yellow colouring (fat soluble)
Seeds of 1 vanilla bean

Put the cocoa butter in a heatproof bowl over a saucepan of simmering water and stir occasionally until melted. Blend in the colouring until the coating resembles the colour of a green pear, then add the vanilla seeds. Transfer the mixture to a jug and set aside.

ASSEMBLY

Dark cocoa powder, for dusting

Check that the cocoa butter coating is between 40°C (104°F) and 45°C (113°F). If necessary, reheat the dip in 10–20 seconds bursts in the microwave.

Remove the frozen pears from the moulds and patch up any air bubbles with the left-over ganache. Use your palms to smooth the outside of the pears.

Carefully insert a skewer through the top of one of the pears, ensuring it is secure. Dip the pear into the coating until completely submerged, then lift it up, scraping the bottom on the edge of the jug to flatten it, and place on a silicone mat to dry. Remove the skewer and insert a chocolate twig into the hole. Repeat with the remaining pears. Place the pears in the fridge to thaw before serving.

Finish by lightly brushing a little cocoa powder on one side of the pears.

PEAR & YUZU WHIPPED GANACHE: Push one of the frozen pear inserts down into each of the ganache-filled moulds.

ASSEMBLY: Carefully dip each pear into the cocoa butter coating until it is completely submerged.

MAGIC MUSHROOMS

Magic to your eyes and your tastebuds, not so much to your psychedelic mind! Mushrooms have a unique, rich umami flavour and are quite versatile, even when used in a dessert. I think the earthiness of mushrooms pairs perfectly with deep, nutty, roasted flavours such as coffee, chocolate, caramel and hazelnut.

COFFEE CHOCOLATE CRÉMEUX MUSHROOM STALKS

150 ml (5 fl oz) full-cream milk
150 ml (5 fl oz) single (pure) cream
2 eggs
10 g (¼ oz) white (granulated) sugar
200 g (7 oz) milk chocolate
3 g (⅛ oz) freeze-dried coffee granules

Combine the milk and cream in a saucepan and bring to the boil.

Meanwhile, whisk the eggs and sugar in a heatproof bowl until fluffy. Whisk in the hot milk mixture, then pour the mixture back into the pan and cook until it reaches 83°C (181°F) on a sugar thermometer. Add the chocolate and coffee and whisk until melted and smooth. Strain the crémeux into a container and refrigerate overnight.

Cut eight 6 cm (2½ inch) squares of acetate. Roll each square to form a cone with a 3 cm (1¼ inch) diameter as shown below and secure it with tape. Place the cones in a container on a bed of raw quinoa or rice to hold them upright. Pipe the crémeux into the cones until they are almost full. Place the container in the freezer until the crémeux is frozen solid. Remove the acetate and return the cones to the freezer. →

COFFEE CHOCOLATE CRÉMEUX MUSHROOM STALKS: Roll each acetate square into a small cone and secure it with tape.

Stand the acetate cones upright in a container of raw quinoa or rice and pipe the crémeux into the cones until they are almost full.

CRÈME PÂTISSIÈRE

250 ml (9 fl oz) full-cream milk
2 egg yolks
55 g (2 oz) caster (superfine) sugar
20 g (¾ oz) cornflour (cornstarch)

Pour the milk into a saucepan and bring it to a simmer.

Meanwhile, whisk the egg yolks and sugar until fluffy, then stir in the cornflour until the mixture is well combined and forms a paste-like consistency.

Whisk the hot milk into the egg yolk mixture, then pour the mixture back into the pan and whisk over medium heat until it has thickened to a very firm custard-like consistency. Immediately use the hot crème pâtissière to make the hazelnut diplomat cream (see below).

HAZELNUT DIPLOMAT CREAM MUSHROOM CAPS

1 gelatine sheet (titanium grade)
1 quantity crème pâtissière
   (see above)
100 g (3½ oz) hazelnut paste
100 g (3½ oz) dark chocolate
300 ml (10½ fl oz) thickened
   (whipping) cream

Soak the gelatine in cold water to soften.

Pour the hot crème pâtissière into a jug. Squeeze the excess water from the softened gelatine and add it to the jug, along with the hazelnut paste and chocolate. Using an immersion blender, blend until the mixture is completely smooth. Transfer the mixture to a bowl and refrigerate for 30–45 minutes or until cool.

Whisk the cream until medium peaks form, then fold it through the crème pâtissière mixture.

Transfer the diplomat cream to a piping bag. Place a 5 cm (2 inch) diameter silicone hemisphere mould on a tray. Pipe the diplomat cream into eight moulds, filling them three-quarters full. Use the back of a spoon to make a small well in the centre of the cream. Place in the freezer until frozen solid. Return the rest of the diplomat cream to the fridge until needed.

NOTE: You'll find hazelnut paste in specialty food stores. Alternatively, you can buy a chocolate hazelnut spread (such as Nutella).

CHOCOLATE SOIL

180 g (6 oz) almond meal
180 g (6 oz) white (granulated) sugar
110 g (3¾ oz) plain (all-purpose) flour
60 g (2¼ oz) dark cocoa powder
Pinch of salt
105 g (3½ oz) unsalted butter
1 egg

Preheat the oven to 170°C (340°F). Line a baking tray with baking paper.

Combine the dry ingredients in a mixer fitted with the paddle attachment and mix on low speed until combined. Add the butter and mix until a sandy texture is formed. Add the egg and mix until a dough is formed.

Transfer the dough onto the baking tray and roll out until it is 1 cm (½ inch) thick. Bake for 15–17 minutes. Allow to cool completely, then break the cooked chocolate dough into pieces and transfer to a food processor. Blend until a crumble is formed. Store in an airtight container.

PORCINI ICE CREAM

500 ml (17 fl oz) full-cream milk
75 ml (2¼ fl oz) thickened (whipping)
   cream
30 g (1 oz) porcini powder
Pinch of salt
5 egg yolks
110 g (3¾ oz) white (granulated)
   sugar
Ice cubes

Combine the milk, cream, porcini powder and salt in a saucepan and cook over medium heat until simmering.

Meanwhile, whisk the egg yolks and sugar until fluffy, then whisk in the hot milk mixture. Pour the mixture back into the pan and whisk over low heat until it reaches 83°C (181°F) on a sugar thermometer.

Sit the saucepan in a bowl of ice to cool the mixture completely, then strain it through a fine sieve and churn it in an ice-cream maker. Store the ice cream in the freezer until needed.

WHITE CHOCOLATE DIP

100 g (3½ oz) white chocolate
100 g (3½ oz) cocoa butter
Dark cocoa powder, for dusting

Combine the white chocolate and cocoa butter in a heatproof bowl over a saucepan of simmering water and stir occasionally until melted. Transfer the dip to a cup and check that it is between 40°C (104°F) and 45°C (113°F).

Push a skewer into one of the frozen crémeux stalks and lower it into the chocolate dip. Brush the chocolate up and down as it's setting to create grooves as shown, then brush the stalk with some cocoa powder. Remove the skewer and stand the stalk in a container. Repeat with the remaining crémeux stalks, then place in the fridge. →

WHITE CHOCOLATE DIP: Dip the frozen crémeux stalks into the white chocolate dip, then brush up and down to create grooves.

Gently brush the chocolate-coated crémeux stalks with a little cocoa powder so that they resemble mushroom stalks.

DARK CHOCOLATE DIP: Carefully push a skewer into the dented centre of one of the frozen mushroom caps.

Lower the rounded side of the mushroom cap into the dark chocolate dip until the dip reaches the edge.

ASSEMBLY: Pipe small dollops of the reserved hazelnut diplomat cream onto a serving plate.

Gently press the mushroom stalks into the diplomat cream to help secure them in place.

DARK CHOCOLATE DIP

100 g (3½ oz) dark chocolate
100 g (3½ oz) cocoa butter

Combine the chocolate and cocoa butter in a heatproof bowl over a saucepan of simmering water and stir occasionally until melted. Transfer the dip to a cup and check that it is between 40°C (104°F) and 45°C (113°F).

Unmould one of the frozen mushroom caps and insert a skewer into the dented centre (see left). Lower the rounded side of the mushroom cap into the dip until it reaches the edge. Allow the excess chocolate to drip off, then remove the skewer. Place the mushroom cap on a tray. Repeat with the remaining mushroom caps. Put the tray in the fridge for 20–25 minutes so the mushroom caps thaw slightly before serving.

ASSEMBLY

Dark cocoa powder, for dusting
Edible flowers, to garnish
Micro herbs, to garnish

Pipe small dollops of diplomat cream onto six serving plates (see left). Press the mushroom stalks into the diplomat cream to secure them. Sprinkle two spoonfuls of the chocolate soil around the base of each mushroom stalk and then carefully stick the mushroom caps on top of the stalks. Dust the mushroom caps with cocoa.

Serve each mushroom with a scoop of the porcini ice cream. Garnish with small dollops of diplomat cream, edible flowers and micro herbs.

SITTING IN THE FOREST

I love nature and nature-inspired dishes, recreating a scene or taking a piece of nature onto a plate. It makes for a fun, interactive experience. This dish was first inspired by Dominique Crenn from Atelier Crenn, when she made a blackforest dessert that included a chocolate tree. I thought the way it was presented was incredible and so I made my own version. I wanted the dish to include a wood flavour, so I steeped oakwood (oak barrel) chips in the milk to make the diplomat cream. It's a unique way to bring an oak flavour to the dish.

ROASTED MILK CHOCOLATE GANACHE

280 g (10 oz) milk chocolate
1 gelatine sheet (titanium grade)
140 ml (4½ fl oz) full-cream milk
200 ml (7 fl oz) thickened (whipping) cream

Preheat the oven to 150°C (300°F). Line a baking tray with baking paper and spread the chocolate on the tray. Roast for 15 minutes or until the cocoa butter has split from the chocolate and the chocolate looks dry.

Meanwhile, soak the gelatine in cold water to soften.

Pour the milk and cream into a saucepan and bring to the boil. Remove from the heat, add the roasted chocolate and use an immersion blender to blend until melted and smooth. Squeeze the excess water from the softened gelatine, add it to the pan and stir until dissolved and well combined.

Transfer the ganache to a container and refrigerate for 4–5 hours, or preferably overnight, until set.

OAKWOOD CRÈME PÂTISSIÈRE

25 g (1 oz) oakwood chips
275 ml (9½ fl oz) full-cream milk
2 egg yolks
55 g (2 oz) white (granulated) sugar
20 g (¾ oz) cornflour (cornstarch)

Preheat the oven to 170°C (340°F). Spread the oakwood chips on a baking tray and bake for 15 minutes.

Pour the milk into a saucepan and add the toasted oakwood chips. Bring to a simmer, then turn off the heat. Pour the mixture into a jug and place in the fridge to steep overnight.

Strain the milk into a saucepan through a very fine sieve and bring it to a simmer.

Meanwhile, whisk the egg yolks and sugar until fluffy, then stir in the cornflour until the mixture is well combined and forms a paste-like consistency.

Whisk the hot milk into the egg yolk mixture, then pour the mixture back into the pan and whisk over medium heat until it has thickened to a very firm custard-like consistency. Immediately use the hot crème pâtissière to make the oakwood diplomat cream (see page 165). →

CHOCOLATE LOG: Spread a thin, even layer of the tempered chocolate over the acetate sheet.

Roll up the acetate sheet to form a chocolate tube with the acetate on the outside.

Once the chocolate is completely set, carefully remove the acetate from the tube.

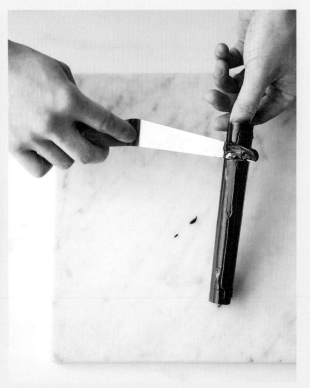

Using an offset spatula, quickly spread some of the tempered chocolate onto the tube to create a bark effect.

OAKWOOD DIPLOMAT CREAM

½ gelatine sheet (titanium grade)
150 g (5½ oz) white chocolate
1 quantity oakwood crème pâtissière
    (see page 162)
300 ml (10½ fl oz) thickened (whipping)
    cream

Soak the gelatine in cold water to soften.

Put the white chocolate in a jug and add the hot crème pâtissière. Squeeze the excess water from the softened gelatine and add it to the jug. Using an immersion blender, blend until the mixture is completely smooth. Transfer the mixture to a bowl and refrigerate for 30–45 minutes or until cool.

Whisk the cream until medium peaks form, then fold it through the crème pâtissière mixture. Place in the fridge until needed.

CHOCOLATE LOG & TREE

300 g (10½ oz) 55% dark chocolate
Ice cubes

Cut a 10 x 16 cm (4 x 6¼ inch) piece of acetate.

Put 200 g (7 oz) of the chocolate in a microwave-safe bowl and microwave on high in 30–40 second bursts, stirring in between, until just melted. Temper the chocolate by adding the rest of the chocolate in batches, cooking each batch in 10 second bursts until melted.

Spread a thin, even layer of chocolate on the acetate (see left) and roll it up to form a 2.5 cm (1 inch) diameter tube with the acetate on the outside. Set aside on a tray, with the cut side of the acetate facing down, until the chocolate is completely set.

Remove the acetate and use an offset spatula to spread the tempered chocolate onto the tube to create the bark of the chocolate log as shown. Work quickly to prevent the tube from melting. Place the log on a tray in the fridge to set.

Meanwhile, transfer the excess tempered chocolate to a piping bag and cut 1 cm (½ inch) off the tip. Pipe a 5 cm (2 inch) length of chocolate into a bowl of iced water, moving back and forth to create the base of the chocolate tree. Slightly raise the base of the tree and continue piping onto it to create branches as you pull the tree through the water. Continue until the chocolate resembles a willow tree. Repeat to make a second tree. *See photographs on page 167.*

Once the chocolate log has set, use a small warm knife to cut it in half to make two 7.5 cm (3 inch) pieces. Place the chocolate logs and trees in the fridge until needed.

PASSIONFRUIT CARAMEL

100 g (3½ oz) white (granulated) sugar
10 g (¼ oz) liquid glucose
20 g (¾ oz) unsalted butter
90 ml (3 fl oz) thickened (whipping)
    cream
Seeds of ½ vanilla bean
1 g (1⁄16 oz) salt
25 ml (¾ fl oz) passionfruit juice

Combine the sugar and glucose in a saucepan. Cook over medium heat, stirring occasionally, until the caramel turns a deep, dark amber.

Whisk in the butter, then slowly whisk in the cream until combined (be careful as it will spit). Simmer for 5 minutes, then add the vanilla seeds, salt and passionfruit juice. Cook until the caramel has reduced and thickened enough to coat the spoon. Remove the pan from the heat and allow the caramel to cool before transferring it to a squeeze bottle. Place in the fridge until needed. ➔

CHOCOLATE SOIL

180 g (6 oz) almond meal
180 g (6 oz) white (granulated) sugar
110 g (3¾ oz) plain (all-purpose)
  flour
60 g (2¼ oz) dark cocoa powder
Pinch of salt
105 g (3½ oz) unsalted butter
1 egg

Preheat the oven to 170°C (340°F). Line a baking tray with baking paper.

Combine the dry ingredients in a mixer fitted with the paddle attachment and mix on low speed until combined. Add the butter and mix until a sandy texture is formed. Add the egg and mix until a dough is formed.

Transfer the dough onto the baking tray and roll out until it is 1 cm (½ inch) thick. Bake for 15–17 minutes. Allow to cool completely, then break the cooked chocolate dough into pieces and transfer to a food processor. Blend until a crumble is formed. Store in an airtight container.

ASSEMBLY

1 lime
Micro mint leaves, to garnish
Bronze fennel, to garnish
Purple shiso leaves, to garnish

Transfer the roasted milk chocolate ganache to a piping bag and pipe it on one end of a chocolate log in a circular motion to create a sealed base (see right). Sit the log in a bowl of the chocolate soil to coat the ganache.

Pour the passionfruit caramel into the centre of the chocolate log to come 2 cm (¾ inch) from the top. Cover with more chocolate ganache and coat the ganache with chocolate soil. Lay the filled log in a container and store in the fridge until needed. Repeat with the second chocolate log.

Transfer the oakwood diplomat cream to a piping bag. Pipe seven dollops of the cream onto each serving plate in an almost straight line and place a chocolate log on top.

Place spoonfuls of the chocolate soil around the chocolate logs. Use a microplane to grate the lime zest and place it on top of the soil. Pipe an extra dollop of ganache next to each chocolate log and secure the willow trees, then add some extra soil around the base. Garnish with the herbs.

CHOCOLATE TREE: Raise the base of the tree, then continue piping onto it to create branches as you pull the tree through the iced water.

Continue piping the chocolate until it resembles a willow tree.

ASSEMBLY: Pipe the roasted milk chocolate ganache onto one end of each chocolate log to create a sealed base.

Arrange the chocolate log, tree and soil on a serving plate, then create a forest scene by adding grated lime zest and micro herbs.

ONYX

Just like the gemstone, this dessert is all about black. I wanted to create a dish with a mysterious look and I think this is pretty sexy! Taking inspiration from my time at Gastro Park and from Grant King's chocolate ball that you cracked open to reveal two types of anglaise, I designed this dish so that once it's broken, vibrant colour spills out. This interaction with the dish makes it such fun to eat.

To make things all black in this dish, I've used activated charcoal powder, which is natural in colour and neutral in taste. You can buy it from health-food stores or online.

SOFT DARK CHOCOLATE GANACHE

1 gelatine sheet (titanium grade)
140 ml (4½ fl oz) full-cream milk
200 ml (7 fl oz) single (pure) cream
280 g (10 oz) dark chocolate

Soak the gelatine in cold water to soften.

Pour the milk and cream into a saucepan and bring to the boil.

Pour the hot cream mixture into a jug with the chocolate and use an immersion blender to blend until well combined. Squeeze the excess water from the softened gelatine, add it to the cream mixture and blend until dissolved and well combined. Transfer the ganache to a container and refrigerate for a few hours, preferably overnight, until set.

MATCHA ANGLAISE

250 ml (9 fl oz) full-cream milk
125 ml (4 fl oz) thickened (whipping) cream
25 g (1 oz) liquid glucose
3 egg yolks
55 g (2 oz) white (granulated) sugar
10 g (¼ oz) matcha powder

Combine the milk, cream and glucose in a saucepan and bring to a simmer over medium heat.

Meanwhile, whisk the egg yolks and sugar in a heatproof bowl until fluffy. Whisk in the hot milk mixture, then pour the mixture back into the pan and stir over medium heat until the anglaise reaches 85°C (185°F) on a sugar thermometer. Pour the mixture into a jug and use an immersion blender to blend in the matcha powder.

Pour the matcha anglaise into four 5 cm (2 inch) diameter silicone hemisphere moulds. Place in the freezer for 4–5 hours or until frozen solid. →

LIME GINGER ANGLAISE

250 ml (9 fl oz) full-cream milk
125 ml (4 fl oz) thickened (whipping)
   cream
25 g (1 oz) liquid glucose
Grated zest of ½ lime
25 g (1 oz) fresh ginger, sliced
3 egg yolks
55 g (2 oz) white (granulated) sugar

Combine the milk, cream, glucose, lime zest and ginger in a saucepan and bring to a simmer over medium heat.

Meanwhile, whisk the egg yolks and sugar in a heatproof bowl until fluffy. Whisk in the hot milk mixture, then pour the mixture back into the pan and stir over medium heat until the anglaise reaches 85°C (185°F) on a sugar thermometer. Remove the pan from the heat and leave to steep for 3 hours.

Strain the lime ginger anglaise into a jug and pour it into four 5 cm (2 inch) diameter silicone hemisphere moulds. Place in the freezer for 4–5 hours or until frozen solid.

CHARCOAL CHOCOLATE DIP

200 g (7 oz) white chocolate
200 g (7 oz) cocoa butter
7 g (⅛ oz) activated charcoal powder
   (approximately)

Combine the white chocolate, cocoa butter and charcoal powder in a heatproof bowl over a saucepan of simmering water and stir occasionally until the chocolate has melted. Add more charcoal powder if the colour of the dip isn't dark enough. Transfer the mixture to a jug and blend with an immersion blender until smooth. Set aside, ensuring that the mixture stays between 40°C (104°F) and 45°C (113°F). If necessary, reheat the dip in 10–20 seconds bursts in the microwave.

Remove the frozen anglaise halves from the moulds. Lightly warm the flat surfaces of the frozen anglaise halves on a warm tray. Working quickly, join the anglaise halves together to make four spheres, using one matcha half and one lime ginger half for each one. While still frozen, skewer one side of each sphere with a bamboo skewer and immediately lower it into the chocolate dip until completely submerged. Allow the excess chocolate to drip off, then remove the skewer and seal the hole with your thumb or a warm knife.

Place the spheres in a container lined with paper towel and transfer them to the fridge to thaw.

CHARCOAL TUILES

100 g (3½ oz) unsalted butter

100 g (3½ oz) plain (all-purpose) flour

80 g (2¾ oz) white (granulated) sugar

5 g (⅛ oz) activated charcoal powder

100 g (3½ oz) egg whites

Preheat the oven to 170°C (340°F). Line a baking tray with a silicone baking mat. Cut out a diamond stencil from the lid of a plastic takeaway container (see below).

Melt the butter in a saucepan over low heat.

Meanwhile, combine the flour, sugar and charcoal powder in a mixer fitted with the paddle attachment. Pour in the butter and mix on medium speed until combined. Finally, add the egg whites and mix until a paste is formed.

Spread the tuile mixture over the stencil on the lined baking tray to make several diamond shapes. Bake the tuiles for 8 minutes. As soon as you take them out of the oven, bend and curve them around the handle of a wooden spoon as shown (be careful as they will be hot). Once cooled, store the tuiles in an airtight container until ready to assemble.

NOTE: I highly recommend using a silicone baking mat to line the tray, but you can use baking paper if you don't have one. ➔

CHARCOAL TUILES: Use the diamond stencil to help spread the tuile mixture onto the baking mat.

As soon as the tuiles are cooked, carefully bend and curve each one around the handle of a wooden spoon.

BLACK SESAME SPONGE

40 g (1½ oz) black sesame paste
   (see Note)
3 eggs
1 egg white
60 g (2¼ oz) white (granulated)
   sugar
15 g (½ oz) plain (all-purpose) flour
1 teaspoon activated charcoal
   powder

Use a skewer to poke five holes in the base of a microwave-safe takeaway coffee cup.

Put all of the sponge ingredients in a jug and blend with an immersion blender until combined.

Strain the mixture into a cream whipper and charge twice with N2O. Siphon the mixture into the cup until half full. Microwave the sponge on high for 45 seconds or until the top is dry to the touch. Allow the sponge to cool upside down on a wire rack. *See photographs on page 142.*

NOTE: You can buy black sesame paste from Japanese or Asian grocers.

ASSEMBLY

Transfer the chocolate ganache to a piping bag. Pipe a dollop of ganache in the centre of a serving plate and place one of the chocolate-dipped anglaise spheres on top. Break little pieces of the black sesame sponge and nest them under the sphere.

Pipe little dots of ganache onto one side of the sphere and gently press the charcoal tuiles onto the sphere.

Repeat with the remaining spheres to make four servings. Serve immediately. Eat the onyx by cracking open the chocolate spheres and letting the anglaise ooze out and soak into the sponge.

WHITE NOISE

START THIS RECIPE
A DAY AHEAD

I had the privilege of serving this dessert to Gordon Ramsay in *MasterChef Australia: Back to Win* in 2020. It was a great honour and hearing that he loved the dish felt like a fist bump from a hero, which was an amazing experience.

White Noise offers a sense of purity and wonder. It's inspired by a dessert I had at The Fat Duck in the United Kingdom, an incredible dish that made me want to create as much explosive flavour as possible in something that looks flavourless yet stunning. My version is a little more playful – I've built around fragrant flavours and hidden an intense strawberry gel inside a white chocolate coating.

COCONUT FROZEN PARFAIT

½ gelatine sheet (titanium grade)
100 g (3½ oz) coconut cream
75 g (2½ oz) white chocolate
2 g (1/16 oz) salt
140 ml (4½ fl oz) thickened
  (whipping) cream

Soak the gelatine in cold water to soften.

Combine the coconut cream, white chocolate and salt in a saucepan and stir over medium heat until the chocolate has melted. Squeeze the excess water from the softened gelatine, then add it to the coconut mixture and whisk until dissolved and well combined.

Remove the pan from the heat and whisk in the cream. Pour the mixture into a container and place in the fridge to set overnight.

Cut two 12 x 10 cm (4½ x 4 inch) pieces of acetate and roll each into a 12 x 4.5 cm (4½ x 1¾ inch) tube. Secure each tube with tape, wrap the base with plastic wrap and seal it with tape. Place the tubes in a small jug with the sealed sides at the bottom.

Transfer the coconut mixture to a mixer fitted with the whisk attachment and whisk until medium peaks form. Transfer the mixture to a piping bag and fill the acetate tubes, then gently tap to remove air bubbles. *See photograph on page 177.*

Place the tubes in the freezer for 4–5 hours or until frozen solid, then remove the acetate and cut the parfait into four 6 cm (2½ inch) lengths. Store the parfait in a container in the freezer until needed.

JASMINE TEA ICE CREAM

500 ml (17 fl oz) full-cream milk
75 ml (2¼ fl oz) thickened (whipping)
  cream
30 g (1 oz) jasmine tea leaves
5 egg yolks
110 g (3¾ oz) white (granulated)
  sugar
Ice cubes

Combine the milk, cream and tea leaves in a saucepan and cook over medium heat until simmering.

Meanwhile, whisk the egg yolks and sugar until fluffy, then whisk in the hot milk mixture. Pour the mixture back into the pan and whisk over low heat until it reaches 83°C (181°F) on a sugar thermometer.

Sit the pan in a bowl of ice to cool the mixture completely, then strain it through a fine sieve and churn it in an ice-cream maker. Store in the freezer until needed.

NOTE: Instead of boiling the jasmine tea with the milk, you can just steep it in the fridge overnight and this will keep the ice cream as white as possible. →

WHITE CHOCOLATE CRUMBLE

50 g (1¾ oz) white chocolate
20 g (¾ oz) maltodextrin

Melt the white chocolate in a heatproof bowl in the microwave or over a saucepan of simmering water.

Slowly whisk in the maltodextrin, one spoonful at a time. The mixture should resemble a very light and soft crumble. Place the crumble in the fridge to set (it will become solid).

STRAWBERRY GUM JELLY

200 ml (7 fl oz) water
90 g (3¼ oz) white (granulated) sugar
5 g (⅛ oz) strawberry gum powder
3 g (⅛ oz) konjac powder

Combine the water, sugar and strawberry gum powder in a saucepan. Bring to the boil, then strain the mixture through a very fine sieve. Whisk in the konjac powder. Pour the mixture back into the pan and bring to the boil.

Pour the jelly into a shallow 15 x 5 cm (6 x 2 inch) tray and place in the fridge for 5–10 minutes or until set.

Remove the set jelly from the tray and use a 2.5 cm (1 inch) round cutter to cut out eight circles.

STRAWBERRY CONSOMMÉ GELS

500 g (1 lb 2 oz) frozen strawberries
500 ml (17 fl oz) water
200 g (7 oz) white (granulated) sugar
Seeds of ½ vanilla bean
1.5 g (¹⁄₁₆ oz) citric acid
3 g (⅛ oz) agar

Line a metal tray with a sheet of acetate and place the tray in the freezer.

Combine the strawberries, water, sugar, vanilla seeds and citric acid in a saucepan over low heat. Simmer for 30–45 minutes or until the strawberries are pale and soft. Strain the strawberry mixture into a clean saucepan through a fine sieve without pressing the pulp.

Cook the strained mixture until reduced and slightly thickened. It should be a deep red colour and have a very intense strawberry flavour. Whisk in the agar and bring to the boil. Pour the consommé into a container and place in the fridge for 15–20 minutes or until completely set.

Cut the strawberry consommé into rough cubes, then place them in a blender and blend until smooth.

Spoon 1.5–2 cm (⅝–¾ inch) dollops of the strawberry gel onto the cold metal tray (see right). Return the tray to the freezer for 2–3 hours or until the gels are frozen.

WHITE CHOCOLATE DIP

150 g (5½ oz) white chocolate
150 g (5½ oz) cocoa butter

Combine the white chocolate and cocoa butter in a heatproof bowl over a saucepan of simmering water and stir occasionally until melted. Turn off the heat and leave the bowl sitting over the saucepan to keep the dip warm.

NOTE: Because cocoa butter naturally has a yellow tinge, I add titanium dioxide, an edible white pigment, to create a much purer finish to the chocolate dip.

STRAWBERRY PEBBLES

1 quantity white chocolate dip
  (see above)
1 quantity strawberry consommé
  gels *(see left)*

Line a container with baking paper.

Check the temperature of the white chocolate dip. If needed, gently reheat it over a saucepan of simmering water until it is between 40°C (104°F) and 47°C (117°F). Transfer the dip to a small cup.

Using a toothpick, skewer one of the frozen strawberry gels. Lower it into the dip until fully submerged, then immediately remove it from the dip and allow the chocolate to drip off (the coating will set immediately). Transfer the pebble to the container and remove the toothpick. Seal the hole with a tiny drop of the chocolate dip. Repeat until all the strawberry gels have been dipped.

Transfer the pebbles to a container and place in the fridge until needed. →

COCONUT FROZEN PARFAIT: Pipe the parfait mixture into the acetate tube, filling the tube completely.

STRAWBERRY CONSOMMÉ GELS: Spoon small dollops of strawberry gel onto a cold metal tray, then place in the freezer.

YOGHURT GEL

100 ml (3½ fl oz) full-cream milk
75 ml (2¼ fl oz) thickened (whipping) cream
25 g (1 oz) white (granulated) sugar
2 g (¹⁄₁₆ oz) agar
100 g (3½ oz) Greek yoghurt
Lemon juice, to taste

Put the milk, cream, sugar and agar in a saucepan and lightly whisk to combine. Place the pan over medium heat and continue whisking until the mixture is boiling. Pour the mixture into a heatproof container and allow it to cool, then place in the fridge until set to a jelly.

Cut the jelly into rough cubes and place in a high-speed blender with the yoghurt and lemon juice. Blend until very smooth, then strain the gel into a squeeze bottle through a fine sieve. Place in the fridge until needed.

ASSEMBLY

Pipe a small dollop of yoghurt gel onto four serving plates, a little off centre. Arrange a slice of the coconut parfait on top.

Pipe seven more small dollops of yoghurt gel around and on top of the parfait.

Arrange three strawberry pebbles around the parfait and add two rounds of the strawberry gum jelly.

Place a spoonful of the jasmine tea ice cream directly beside the coconut parfait. Lightly sprinkle the white chocolate crumble over the top.

RED VEIL

Inspired by the colour red, I've used as many red flavours as possible in this dramatic dessert. The red veil reveals a few elements, without giving away too much, so that diners explore their way through the dish — a true culinary adventure. This is a complex dessert, but it's a fun one to make if you're up for the challenge and really want to amaze your friends and family. Or just utilise a few of these components to up your dessert game.

BERGAMOT & PINK PEPPER MERINGUE

115 g (4 oz) egg whites
8 g (⅛ oz) egg white powder
60 g (2¼ oz) white (granulated) sugar
160 ml (5¼ fl oz) bergamot juice
3 g (⅛ oz) pink peppercorns, ground to a fine powder

Place all of the ingredients in a blender and blend until combined. Set aside for 5 minutes to hydrate the egg white powder, then transfer the mixture to a mixer fitted with the whisk attachment and whisk until stiff peaks form.

Spoon the meringue onto a silicone mat and spread until 1.5 cm (⅝ inch) thick. Dehydrate overnight at 70°C (150°F).

Break the dried meringue into 5 cm (2 inch) chunks and store in an airtight container until needed.

NOTE: If you don't have a dehydrator, you can cook the meringue in an 80–90°C (176–194°F) oven instead.

WHITE CHOCOLATE GÉNOISE

115 g (4 oz) white chocolate
95 g (3¼ oz) butter
20 g (¾ oz) Trimoline (*see Note*)
3 egg whites
50 g (1¾ oz) white (granulated) sugar
3 egg yolks
50 g (1¾ oz) plain (all-purpose) flour

Preheat the oven to 170°C (340°F). Line a 20 cm (8 inch) cake tin with baking paper.

Melt the white chocolate, butter and Trimoline in a heatproof bowl in the microwave or over a saucepan of simmering water. Stir until combined.

Meanwhile, combine the egg whites and sugar in a mixer fitted with the whisk attachment and whisk until medium peaks form.

Whisk the egg yolks into the white chocolate mixture, then fold in the flour and the meringue.

Spoon the batter into the cake tin. Bake the génoise for 30–35 minutes or until a skewer inserted into the centre comes out clean. Allow to cool, then cut it into 2.5 cm (1 inch) cubes. Refrigerate the cubes in an airtight container until needed.

NOTE: Trimoline is an invert sugar made of glucose and fructose. You can substitute it with glucose syrup or honey. →

RASPBERRY CONSOMMÉ VEIL

175 g (6 oz) fresh or frozen
    raspberries

175 g (6 oz) fresh or frozen
    strawberries

325 ml (11 fl oz) water

60 g (2¼ oz) white (granulated)
    sugar

3 g (⅛ oz) agar (approximately)

Lightly oil a shallow metal tray.

Combine the berries, water and sugar in a saucepan over medium heat. Bring to a simmer, then cook for 15–25 minutes or until the strawberries are pale and soft.

Strain the berry mixture through a fine sieve. Weigh the liquid and whisk in 1% of the weight in agar. For example, 300 g (10½ oz) of liquid will need 3 g (⅛ oz) of agar. Transfer the mixture to a saucepan and bring to the boil. Pour enough of the consommé mixture into the tray to create a very thin layer. Leave the jelly to set at room temperature.

Cut the jelly into 15 cm (6 inch) squares and use a spatula to carefully remove them from the tray as shown below. Store the jelly sheets in a container, stacked on top of each other (don't worry, they won't stick together). Set aside until needed.

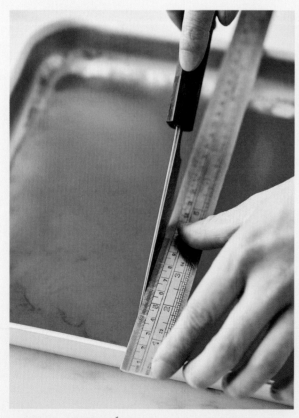

RASPBERRY CONSOMMÉ VEIL: Once the raspberry jelly has set, cut it into four squares.

Carefully peel the jelly sheets off the tray and stack them in a container until needed.

RASPBERRY HIBISCUS SORBET

120 ml (3¾ fl oz) water
65 g (2¼ oz) white (granulated) sugar
25 g (1 oz) liquid glucose
10 g (¼ oz) hibiscus tea leaves
300 g (10½ oz) raspberry purée
3 g (⅛ oz) citric acid

Combine the water, sugar, glucose and tea in a saucepan and bring to a simmer. Remove from the heat and leave to steep for 30 minutes or until cool.

Strain the liquid into a jug and add the raspberry purée and citric acid. Use an immersion blender to blend until well combined.

Churn the mixture in an ice-cream maker, then store in the freezer until needed.

CRÈME PÂTISSIÈRE

250 ml (9 fl oz) full-cream milk
2 egg yolks
55 g (2 oz) caster (superfine) sugar
20 g (¾ oz) cornflour (cornstarch)

Pour the milk into a saucepan and bring it to a simmer.

Meanwhile, whisk the egg yolks and sugar until fluffy, then stir in the cornflour until the mixture is well combined and forms a paste-like consistency.

Whisk the hot milk into the egg yolk mixture, then pour the mixture back into the pan and whisk over medium heat until it has thickened to a very firm custard-like consistency. Immediately use the hot crème pâtissière to make the raspberry diplomat cream (see below).

RASPBERRY DIPLOMAT CREAM

1 gelatine sheet (titanium grade)
1 quantity crème pâtissière
 (see above)
160 g (5½ oz) ruby chocolate
20 g (¾ oz) freeze-dried raspberry
 powder
250 ml (9 fl oz) thickened (whipping)
 cream

Soak the gelatine in cold water to soften.

Pour the hot crème pâtissière into a jug. Squeeze the excess water from the softened gelatine and add it to the jug, along with the ruby chocolate and raspberry powder. Using an immersion blender, blend until the mixture is completely smooth. Transfer the mixture to a bowl and refrigerate for 30–45 minutes or until cool.

Whisk the cream until medium peaks form, then fold it through the crème pâtissière mixture. Place in the fridge until needed.

ASSEMBLY

12 raspberries
3 strawberries, cut into eighths
12 freeze-dried plum slices
Purple linaria flowers, to garnish
Purple shiso leaves, to garnish
Elderflower sprigs, to garnish

Transfer the raspberry diplomat cream to a piping bag. Place three génoise cubes close together on a serving plate. Pipe five dollops of the diplomat cream randomly around and on top of the cubes. Add two more génoise cubes. Add three raspberries and five strawberry pieces, sticking them in between the gaps of the génoise and on top of the diplomat cream. Arrange three freeze-dried plum slices on the diplomat cream and add three of the bergamot meringue chunks. Rocher the raspberry hibiscus sorbet in the middle of the génoise stack. *See photographs on page 189.*

Gently drape the raspberry consommé veil over the top. Garnish with the linaria, purple shiso and elderflower. Serve immediately.

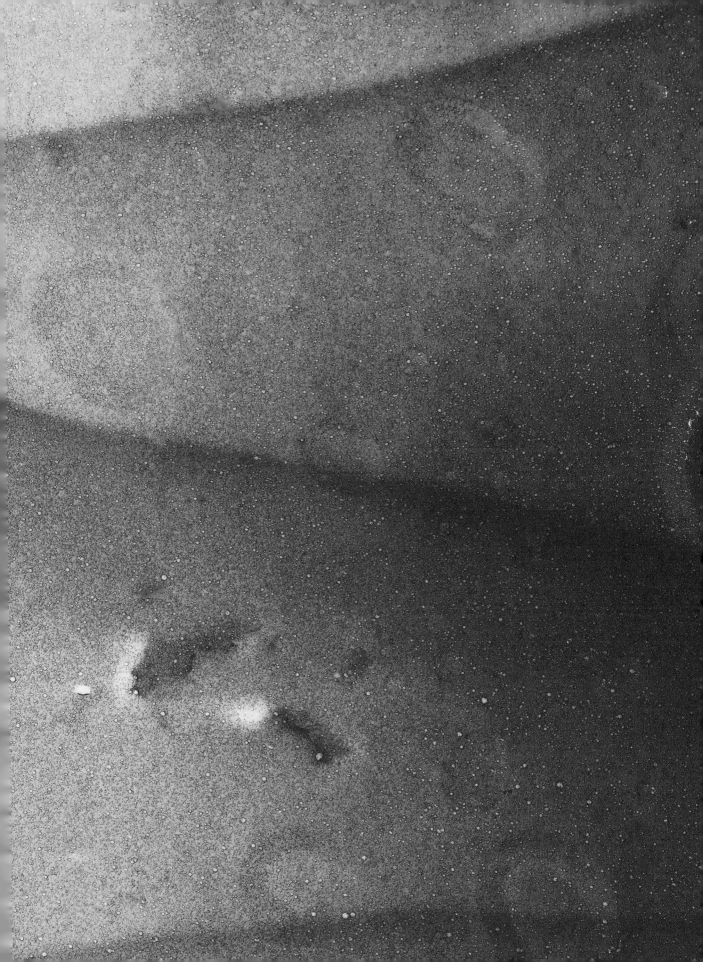

PURPLE

When I first set out to create a monochrome menu, I was hit with a writer's block that lasted for months. I finally came up with something that had the potential to evolve over time and some day become an epic dessert. It was a huge relief and completely satisfying. Purple has so many different techniques and a combination of flavours that makes it intriguing to eat and even to make.

This is one of my favourites because it looks so stunning and tastes so beautiful. A little disclaimer: it's quite a difficult and complex recipe that will impress your friends, but don't make it at the last minute or you'll set yourself up for failure. Be prepared and take your time. Or make just a few of the components. And if you do end up rushing, just chuck everything into a nice cup to make a trifle!

MIXED BERRY GLASS

150 g (5½ oz) blackberries
150 g (5½ oz) raspberries
150 g (5½ oz) strawberries
200 ml (7 fl oz) water
85 g (3 oz) white (granulated) sugar
3 g (⅛ oz) agar (approximately)

Combine the berries, water and sugar in a saucepan over medium heat. Bring to a simmer, then cook for 15–20 minutes or until the liquid has reduced and the strawberries are pale and soft.

Strain the berry mixture through a fine sieve. Weigh the liquid and add 1% of the weight in agar. For example, 300 g (10½ oz) of liquid will need 3 g (⅛ oz) of agar. Transfer the mixture to a saucepan and bring to the boil. Pour the mixture into a container and place in the fridge for 15–20 minutes or until completely set.

Cut the jelly into rough cubes and place them in a blender. Blend on high speed until smooth, then strain the gel through a sieve. Spread the gel onto an acetate sheet, as thinly as possible. Dehydrate overnight at 60°C (140°F).

Break the mixed berry glass into shards, about 5–7 cm (2–2¾ inches) long. Store in an airtight container.

NOTE: If you don't have a dehydrator, you can dry the glass in an 80°C (176°F) oven on a silicone mat for 4–6 hours.

CASSIS MERINGUE

115 g (4 oz) egg whites
8 g (⅛ oz) egg white powder
60 g (2¼ oz) white (granulated) sugar
160 g (5½ oz) blackcurrant (cassis) purée
40 ml (1¼ fl oz) lemon juice

Place all of the ingredients in a blender and blend until combined. Set aside for 5 minutes to hydrate the egg white powder.

Transfer the mixture to a mixer fitted with the whisk attachment and whisk until stiff peaks form.

Spoon the meringue onto a silicone mat and spread until 1 cm (½ inch) thick. Dehydrate overnight at 60°C (140°F).

Break the dried cassis meringue into pieces. Store in an airtight container.

NOTE: If you don't have a dehydrator, you can cook the meringue in an 80–90°C (176–194°F) oven instead. ➔

CASSIS PARFAIT

1 gelatine sheet (titanium grade)
650 ml (22½ fl oz) thickened
   (whipping) cream
90 g (3¼ oz) white chocolate
100 g (3½ oz) blackcurrant (cassis)
   purée

Soak the gelatine in cold water to soften.

Pour half the cream into a saucepan and heat until simmering. Transfer the hot cream to a jug, add the white chocolate and use an immersion blender to blend until melted and smooth. Squeeze the excess water from the softened gelatine, add it to the chocolate and cream mixture and stir until dissolved and well combined. Set aside to cool for about 10 minutes.

Stir the remaining cream and the blackcurrant purée into the cooled chocolate and cream mixture. Place in the fridge for a few hours until firm.

Warm a well-rounded spoon with hot water. Shake off the excess water, then rocher the cassis parfait mixture onto a tray lined with baking paper, as shown below. Push onto each rocher with the back of the spoon to create a well. Place in the freezer until needed. →

CASSIS PARFAIT: Using a well-rounded hot spoon, scoop into the parfait mixture and twist your wrist as you lift up to form a rocher.

Gently release the cassis parfait rocher onto a baking tray lined with baking paper.

BLACKBERRY LONG PEPPER SORBET

1 kg (2 lb 4 oz) blackberry purée
3 Javanese long peppers, grated
50 g (1¾ oz) Perfecta (50) sorbet
    stabiliser
150 ml (5 fl oz) water
50 g (1¾ oz) white (granulated) sugar
Juice of 1 lemon

Combine all the ingredients in a blender and blend until well combined.

Churn the mixture in an ice-cream maker, then store in the freezer until needed.

BLACKBERRY UMESHU GEL

300 g (10½ oz) fresh or frozen
    blackberries
200 ml (7 fl oz) water
100 g (3½ oz) white (granulated)
    sugar
3 g (⅛ oz) gellan gum 'F' low acyl
    (approximately)
90 ml (3 fl oz) umeshu liqueur
1.8 g (¹⁄₁₆ oz) citric acid

Combine the blackberries, water and sugar in a saucepan over medium heat. Bring to a simmer, then cook for 15–20 minutes or until the liquid has reduced and the berries are soft.

Strain the blackberry mixture through a fine sieve. Weigh the liquid and blend in 1% of the weight in gellan gum. For example, 300 g (10½ oz) of liquid would need 3 g (⅛ oz) of gellan gum. Transfer the mixture to a saucepan and bring to the boil. Pour into a container and refrigerate for 15–20 minutes or until set to a firm jelly.

Cut the jelly into rough cubes and place them in a blender. Blend on high speed until smooth, then add the umeshu liqueur and citric acid and blend again. Strain the gel through a fine sieve, then transfer it to a piping bag and place in the fridge.

WHITE CHOCOLATE BERRY MALTO

200 g (7 oz) white chocolate
15 g (½ oz) maltodextrin
    (approximately)
50 g (1¾ oz) freeze-dried
    blackberries

Put the white chocolate in a heatproof bowl over a saucepan of simmering water and stir occasionally until melted. Whisk in enough maltodextrin until the mixture has dried into clumps and has the consistency of a light crumble. Place in the fridge to set for 30 minutes.

Transfer the mixture to a Thermomix or high-speed blender and blend in the freeze-dried blackberries. Transfer the mixture to a container and set aside.

ASSEMBLY

Freeze-dried blackberries, to garnish
Purple linaria or other edible purple
    flowers, to garnish

Pipe some of the blackberry gel in the centre of eight serving plates. Place a rocher of the cassis parfait on top of the gel. Sprinkle the white chocolate berry malto over the parfait. Place a rocher of the blackberry sorbet on top of the parfait, then place two large shards of the berry glass on each side. Place broken pieces of the cassis meringue on top of the sorbet.

Pipe dots of blackberry gel randomly onto the parfait and plate. Garnish with the freeze-dried blackberries and flowers.

PASSION BERRY CHEESECAKE SLICE

Here's a cheesecake recipe that will surely impress. It combines a cheesecake mousse with a lime ganache, blueberry jelly and passionfruit curd. It's quite a lengthy recipe and a time-consuming process, but the results are stunning and well worth the effort, especially for a celebration or special gathering. The hard work and dedication shows through every layer.

WHEAT BISCUIT BASE

125 g (4½ oz) wheat biscuits, crushed
40 g (1½ oz) unsalted butter, melted

Line a baking tray with baking paper. Place a 36 x 16 cm (14¼ x 6¼ inch) rectangular stainless steel pastry frame on the tray.

Combine the crushed biscuits and melted butter in a bowl. Tip the mixture into the pastry frame and then press down firmly with an offset palette knife to make it completely flat. Place in the freezer to set.

LIME GANACHE

150 ml (5 fl oz) single (pure) cream
150 g (5½ oz) white chocolate
35 ml (1 fl oz) lime juice
20 g (¾ oz) unsalted butter

Pour the cream into a saucepan and cook over medium heat until simmering. Add the white chocolate, lime juice and butter and whisk until well combined.

Pour a thin layer of ganache into the pastry frame over the wheat biscuit base. Transfer to the freezer until needed.

CHEESECAKE MOUSSE

1 gelatine sheet (titanium grade)
230 g (8 oz) cream cheese, softened
60 g (2¼ oz) white (granulated) sugar
Grated zest and juice of 1 lemon
140 ml (4½ fl oz) thickened (whipping) cream

Soak the gelatine in cold water to soften.

Beat the cream cheese and sugar in a mixer fitted with the whisk attachment until combined. Whisk in the lemon zest and lemon juice. Squeeze the excess water from the softened gelatine, add it to the cream cheese mixture and whisk until dissolved and well combined. Fold in the cream.

Spread half of the mousse over the lime ganache in an even layer. Put the remaining mousse in the fridge until needed. Return the cheesecake to the freezer while you prepare the blueberry jelly. →

BLUEBERRY JELLY

1 gelatine sheet (titanium grade)
75 g (2½ oz) blueberry purée
15 g (½ oz) white (granulated) sugar
45 ml (1½ fl oz) water

Soak the gelatine in cold water to soften.

Combine the blueberry purée, sugar and water in a saucepan. Squeeze the excess water from the softened gelatine and add it to the pan. Cook over low heat until the gelatine has just dissolved.

Pour the jelly on top of the cheesecake mousse in an even layer, then return it to the freezer to set, ensuring it is level.

Once the jelly is frozen, spread the remaining cheesecake mousse on top of the jelly, ensuring it is level, then transfer to the freezer to set.

PASSIONFRUIT CURD

100 ml (3½ fl oz) strained fresh passionfruit juice
65 g (2¼ oz) butter
1 gelatine sheet (titanium grade)
4 eggs
100 g (3½ oz) white (granulated) sugar

Combine the passionfruit juice and butter in a saucepan. Cook over medium heat until simmering.

Meanwhile, soak the gelatine in cold water to soften.

Whisk the eggs and sugar in a heatproof bowl until fluffy, then whisk in the hot passionfruit mixture. Place the bowl over a saucepan of simmering water and cook, whisking continually, until the mixture is thick. Squeeze the excess water from the softened gelatine, add it to the passionfruit mixture and whisk until dissolved and well combined.

Strain the hot passionfruit curd mixture into a jug and blend with an immersion blender. Set aside until cool.

Spoon small amounts of the passionfruit curd evenly over the cheesecake mousse and spread it out to make a thin layer of curd. There should be 5 mm (¼ inch) of space left at the top of the pastry frame. Return the cheesecake to the freezer.

Transfer any excess passionfruit curd into a piping bag.

NOTE: Any left-over passionfruit curd can be stored in the fridge for up to 4 weeks, or frozen for a few months.

LIME JELLY

2 gelatine sheets (titanium grade)
100 ml (3½ fl oz) water
75 ml (2¼ fl oz) lime juice
50 g (1¾ oz) white (granulated) sugar

Soak the gelatine in cold water to soften.

Meanwhile, combine the water, lime juice and sugar in a saucepan and bring to a simmer. Squeeze the excess water from the softened gelatine, add it to the pan and whisk until dissolved and well combined. Set aside to cool to room temperature.

Pour the jelly over the frozen passionfruit curd to create a thin layer, approximately 1.5–2 mm (about 1/16 inch) thick. Return the cheesecake to the freezer one last time until frozen solid.

CHANTILLY CREAM

100 ml (3½ fl oz) thickened
  (whipping) cream
25 g (1 oz) white (granulated) sugar

Combine the cream and sugar in a mixer fitted with the whisk attachment and whisk until stiff peaks form.

Transfer the chantilly cream to a piping bag and store it in the fridge until needed.

ASSEMBLY

Liquid glucose
Edible flowers, to garnish
Micro mint, to garnish
Blueberries or raspberries,
  to garnish

Gently warm the outside of the pastry frame with a blowtorch to help release it. Warm a long sharp knife in hot water, then wipe the knife and trim the edges of the cheesecake. Using a ruler as a guide, cut the cheesecake into 3 x 12 cm (1¼ x 4½ inch) slices, heating and wiping the knife after each cut. Transfer to the fridge to thaw before serving.

Spread a little liquid glucose on each serving plate to secure the cheesecake slice.

Pipe dollops of passionfruit curd and chantilly cream on top of the lime jelly and garnish with the flowers, mint and halved berries.

Serve immediately or store in an airtight container in the fridge for up to 3–5 days.

SPECIALTY INGREDIENTS

- **Activated charcoal powder:** A black powder made of activated charcoal, often used in a health context to absorb toxins. I use it for its natural colour.
- **Agar:** A setting agent derived from red seaweed, used to make firm jellies or gels, as well as brittle jellies or 'glass'. Available in Asian grocers or health-food stores.
- **Bergamot juice:** The juice of a citrus fruit native to southern Italy. Look for it in health-food stores or online.
- **Black sesame paste:** A paste made from black sesame seeds, sweetened with honey. Found in Asian grocers.
- **Citric acid:** A weak acid extracted from citrus fruits (sometimes manufactured). I use it as a flavouring agent and treat it the same way as I would treat salt.
- **Cocoa butter:** The fat extracted from cocoa beans. Sold in specialty hospitality stores.
- **Edible flowers:** I use linaria, violas, elderflowers and alyssum. Buy them from local markets and growers.
- **Freeze-dried coffee (instant coffee):** Espresso coffee that has been processed into dried granules.
- **Freeze-dried fruit:** Adds crunch and fruit flavour. Look for it in health-food stores or specialty hospitality stores (I like the New Zealand brand Fresh As).
- **Fruit purées:** I use purées from Boiron, a French company, as they regulate the level of sweetness, making the flavour very consistent. You can make your own, but you'll need to adjust the sweetness.
- **Fat-soluble colouring:** A food-grade colouring dissolves in fat, making it ideal for colouring chocolate or cocoa butter.
- **Edible gold dust/Gold lustre:** A food-grade edible gold powder, available in cake decorating stores or specialty hospitality stores.

- **Gelatine sheet (titanium grade):** An almost odourless and flavourless gelling agent that's used for creating jellies and setting mousses.
- **Gellan gum:** A food additive used to bind, stabilise and texturise processed foods. Look for it online or in specialty hospitality stores.
- **Jackfruit:** An exotic tropical fruit with a sweet banana- and apple-like flavour. It can be quite pungent and has a meaty texture. Available canned or frozen in Asian grocers.
- **Javanese long peppers:** Native to Indonesia, these resemble a rough, short tail. They have a sweet, fragrant, musk-like aroma and are available from specialist spice retailers.
- **Konjac powder:** Derived from a tuber and used to create jellies or thicken foods. Sold in Asian supermarkets.
- **Liquid glucose:** A thick, clear syrup that's often used in chocolate and confectionery making. It helps keep foods soft and moist.
- **Maltodextrin:** A white powder made from corn, rice, wheat or potato starch. In dessert making, it's used to absorb fat. Sold in specialty hospitality stores.
- **Matcha powder:** A powdered Japanese green tea used commonly for drinking or baking. Available in Asian grocers.
- **Micro herbs:** Used for decorating and garnishing. I use fennel (regular and bronze), buckler sorrel, mint and shiso (purple and red). Look for them at your local farmer's market.
- **Muscovado sugar:** An unrefined cane sugar that contains natural molasses.
- **Palm sugar (jaggery):** A sugar derived from the sap of the palm tree.
- **Pandan extract:** A green concentrate made from pandan leaves. Found in Asian grocers.

- **Pectin NH powder:** Used to create fruit glazes or jams, and also known as apple pectin. Available in health-food stores and specialty hospitality stores.
- **Perfecta (50):** A sorbet stabiliser made by Comprital. Stabilisers vary between brands, so check the packet instructions if you're using a different brand. Sold in specialty hospitality stores.
- **Pistachio paste:** A paste made of processed pistachios. Use a really good-quality paste made from 100% pistachios as it will affect the flavour and colour of the end product. Sold in specialty hospitality stores or online.
- **Porcini powder:** Dried porcini mushrooms that have been processed into powder.
- **Praline paste:** A sweet paste made from hazelnuts mixed with caramel and blended until smooth. You can create your own and use any nuts you like, as long as you have a high-speed blender. Otherwise, you can substitute Nutella.
- **Sago pearls:** Pearl-like balls prepared from the pith of the sago palm.
- **Strawberry gum powder:** Dried, ground leaves of a native Australian plant that has a flavour profile of strawberries and bubblegum.
- **Trimoline:** An invert sugar made of glucose and fructose. You can substitute it with liquid glucose or honey.
- **Verjuice:** A highly acidic juice made from unripe grapes.
- **Wood chips:** Wood chips from specific trees have different sweet, earthy and smoky flavours. I roast them and steep them in milk and then strain it before using to add a rounded, earthy tone to desserts. Buy them in barbecue stores.
- **Yuzu juice:** The juice of a fragrant Japanese/Korean citrus fruit. Available in Asian grocers.

KITCHEN TOOLS

Here are the key kitchen tools you'll need in order to succeed in the dessert game.

- **Acetate sheet:** This clear, flexible, non-stick plastic sheet is thicker than paper and has many uses. Spread tempered chocolate onto acetate to create a shiny surface, use it to make a stencil template, or to create a temporary tube or cone mould. Look for acetate in art supplies stores or specialty hospitality stores.
- **Blow torch:** A butane-gas fuelled torch that has a flint attachment. It allows for quick cooking or browning.
- **Cream whipper/siphon gun:** A dispenser that uses nitrous-oxide filled metal bulbs or 'cream chargers' to aerate liquids. It's commonly used to whip cream. I also use it to create foams and microwave sponges.
- **Dehydrator:** A versatile tool for drying fruits and meringues. It's also useful for keeping dry items that are prone to absorbing moisture.
- **High-speed blender/food processor:** A blender that's powerful enough to vortex liquids. I use a Thermomix for creating gels or pulverising crumbs.
- **Immersion hand blender:** You'll need this for blending smaller-volume mixtures, such as gels or crémeux.
- **Melon baller:** A small, hemisphere-shaped spoon that's designed to be pressed into the flesh of a melon and rotated in order to cut out spheres of melon.
- **Metal wire rack:** For cooling baked items and also useful when glazing.
- **Mixing bowls:** It's handy to have a range of sizes of metal or microwave-safe glass bowls.
- **Pastry brush:** A nylon or silicone brush used for brushing, spreading or glazing.
- **Pastry frame:** You'll need a stainless steel 15 cm (6 inch) square cake frame that's 5 cm (2 inches) high and a 36 x 16 cm (14¼ x 6¼ inch) rectangular frame.

- **Perforated tart rings:** A metal tart ring with small holes pierced through to allow even airflow and consistent cooking. You'll need a 17 cm (6½ inch) ring and a 20 cm (8 inch) ring
- **Piping bags:** Use reusable piping bags or biodegradable disposable piping bags.
- **Piping nozzles:** A set of round, star and petal piping tips will come in handy.
- **Ramekins and dariole moulds:** It's best to use ceramic or metal moulds.
- **Round cutters:** A set of varying sizes will come in handy.
- **Silicone mat:** A flexible sheet made of food-grade silicone, used for baking. I consider this a must-have – it helps with sugar work, chocolate making, mousse and most baking. I generally it instead of baking paper to line baking trays.
- **Silicone moulds:** These can be purchased online and are very handy when it comes to mass production. Below are the moulds I've used in this book (although they're not all strictly necessary, I do recommend getting the hemisphere mould as it is very versatile):
  - Pavoni 50 mm (2 inch) hemisphere mould
  - Pavoni 25 mm (1 inch) sphere mould
  - Pavoni pear mould
  - Silikomart 65 mm (2½ inch) stone mould
  - Silikomart 50 mm (2 inch) mini muffin mould
  - Flower mould
- **Skewers:** Metal or bamboo skewers are useful for dipping items into melted chocolate.
- **Spring-form cake tins:** Cake tins with removable sides that detach from the base. You'll need 10 cm (4 inch) cake tins and an 18 cm (7 inch) cake tin. They're not essential, but will make life a lot easier when you're baking cakes.
- **Stand mixer:** This will help you with your whipping, folding and mixing. Make sure you have all the attachments.

INDEX

A

Achatz, Grant 7
activated charcoal powder 198
    Onyx 168–173
agar 198
almonds
    Bali sunrise 134–138
    Blackforest jar 100–104
    Chocolate choux 40
    Magic mushrooms 154–159
    Moss 140–145
    Opera 120–124
    Orange blossom ice-cream sandwich
        with lime curd 58–61
    Sitting in the forest 162–167
    A slice of Irish Cream 74–78
    Watermelon jar 70–73
anglaise
    Lime ginger anglaise 170
    Matcha anglaise 168
apples
    Apple caramel 51
    An apple a day 146–149
    Moss 140–145
    Spiced apple pavlovas 48–51
applewood chips 198
    An apple a day 146–149

B

Baileys Irish Cream liqueur
    A slice of Irish Cream 74–78
    Crème caramel 20
Bali sunrise 134–138
bananas: Rum ba-banana & pineapple
    54–57
bergamot juice 198
    Red veil 180–183
berries
    Blackforest jar 100–104
    Boozy berry pavlovas 52
    Mr Grey 80–83
    Passion berry cheesecake slice
        194–197
    Purple 186–191
    Red veil 180–183
    Ruby raspberry & rose tart 92–95

Strawberries & cream 96–99
Watermelon jar 70–73
White noise 174–179
The best basic butter cake 30
black sesame paste 198
    Onyx 168–173
blackberries: Purple 186–191
blackcurrant: Purple 186–191
Blackforest jar 100–104
blueberries
    Boozy berry pavlovas 52
    Passion berry cheesecake slice
        194–197
Boozy berry pavlovas 52
bourbon: Boozy berry pavlovas 52
brownies 11
    Brownie 18
    Brownie base 133
    Chocolate brownie 74, 100
Burnt honey basque cheesecake 22
butter cake: The best basic butter
    cake 30
buttercream: Coffee buttercream 123

C

cake
    The best basic butter cake 30
    Black sesame sponge 173
    Burnt honey basque cheesecake 22
    Chocolate lava s'mores 84–87
    Hazelnut sponge 91
    Opera 120–124
    Passion berry cheesecake slice
        194–197
    Pistachio sponge 142
    Rum ba-banana & pineapple 54–57
    White chocolate génoise 180
caramel
    Apple caramel 51, 149
    Crème caramel 20
    Mille-tuile 110–113
    Moss 140–145
    Nomtella 130–133
    Passionfruit caramel 165
    The ultimate praline tart 114–18
cassis *see* blackcurrant
cendol 7, 134

chantilly cream 197
    Crème fraîche & lime chantilly 57
    Elderflower chantilly 52
charcoal powder 198
    Onyx 168–173
Chardonnay mousse 62
cheesecake
    Burnt honey basque cheesecake 22
    Passion berry cheesecake slice
        194–197
cherries
    Blackforest jar 100–104
    Cherry & coconut pavlovas 47
Chia seed syrup 70
chocolate 10
    see also ruby chocolate, white
        chocolate
    Bali sunrise 134–138
    Blackforest jar 100–104
    Brownie 18
    Cherry & coconut pavlovas 47
    Chocolate choux 40–43
    Chocolate lava s'mores 84–87
    Chocolate mousse 26
    Magic mushrooms 154–159
    Nomtella 130–133
    Onyx 168–173
    Opera 120–124
    Pear & yuzu 150–152
    Sitting in the forest 162–167
    A slice of Irish Cream 74–78
    Tiramisu jar 88–91
    The ultimate praline tart 114–18
choux: Chocolate choux 40–43
Cinnamon pavlovas 48
Citrus meringue tart 36–39
coconut
    Bali sunrise 134–138
    Cherry & coconut pavlovas 47
    Tropical panna cotta jar 106–109
    White noise 174–179
coffee
    Magic mushrooms 154–159
    Nomtella 130–133
    Opera 120–124
    A slice of Irish Cream 74–78
    Tiramisu jar 88–91
    The ultimate praline tart 114–18

compote

Apple compote 149

Berry compote 92

Cherry compote 47, 103

craquelin: Chocolate craquelin 40

cream

An apple a day 146–149

Bali sunrise 134–138

Blackforest jar 100–104

Boozy berry pavlovas 52

Burnt honey basque cheesecake 22

Cherry & coconut pavlovas 47

Chocolate choux 40

Chocolate lava s'mores 84–87

Chocolate mousse 26

Magic mushrooms 154–159

Matcha & yuzu ganache tart 34

Mille-tuile 110–113

Moss 140–145

Mr Grey 80–83

Nomtella 130–133

Onyx 168–173

Opera 120–124

Orange blossom ice-cream sandwich
    with lime curd 58–61

Passion berry cheesecake slice
    194–197

Pear & yuzu 150–152

Purple 186–191

Red veil 180–183

Ruby raspberry & rose tart 92–95

Sitting in the forest 162–167

A slice of Irish Cream 74–78

Spiced apple pavlovas 48–51

Strawberries & cream 96–99

Tiramisu jar 88–91

Tropical panna cotta jar 106–109

The ultimate praline tart 114–18

Vin & grapes 62

White noise 174–179

cream cheese

Burnt honey basque cheesecake 22

Passion berry cheesecake slice
    194–197

Crème caramel 20

Crème fraîche & lime chantilly 57

Crème pâtissière 70, 103, 117, 143,
    156, 183

Applewood crème pâtissière 146

French Earl Grey crème pâtissière 80

Oakwood crème pâtissière 162

crémeux 13

Chocolate crémeux 40

Coffee chocolate crémeux
    mushroom stalks 154

Dark chocolate crémeux 47

Dulce crémeux 40

Ruby crémeux 92

Crenn, Dominique 162

crumble

Sablé crumble 73

Strawberry crumble 83

White chocolate crumble 176

curd 12

Citrus curd 36

Lime curd 61

Passionfruit curd 106, 196

Custard 20

D

dip

Charcoal chocolate dip 170

Chocolate dip 137

Cocoa butter coating 152

Dark chocolate dip 159

Matcha dip 145

White chocolate dip 157, 177

diplomat cream 13

Applewood diplomat cream 146

Blackforest diplomat cream 103

French Earl Grey diplomat
    cream 80

Hazelnut diplomat cream
    mushroom caps 156

Lychee diplomat cream 73

Oakwood diplomat cream 165

Peanut butter diplomat
    cream 117

Raspberry diplomat cream 183

Dulce crémeux 40

E

Earl Grey tea 198

Citrus meringue tart 36–39

Mr Grey 80–83

Ruby raspberry & rose tart 92–95

eclairs 43

elderflower syrup

Boozy berry pavlovas 52

Strawberries & cream 96–99

G

ganache

Chocolate lava s'mores 84–87

Hazelnut ganache 77

Jasmine chocolate ganache 122

Lime ganache 194

Matcha & yuzu ganache tart 34

Pear & yuzu whipped ganache 150

Roasted milk chocolate ganache
    114, 162

Salted vanilla whipped ganache
    48, 110

Soft dark chocolate ganache 168

gel

Blackberry umeshu gel 191

Caramel gel 140

Mango gel 106

Pandan gel 134

Strawberry consommé gels 176

Yoghurt gel 179

gellan gum 198

ginger: Onyx 168–173

glass: Mixed berry glass 186

glaze

Chocolate glaze 133

Dark chocolate glaze 124

granita: Strawberry granita 96

grapes: Vin & grapes 62

H

hazelnuts

Brownie 18

Magic mushrooms 154–159

Nomtella 130–133

A slice of Irish Cream 74–78

Tiramisu jar 88–91

The ultimate praline tart 114–18

hibiscus tea: Red veil 180–183

honey

Burnt honey basque cheesecake 22

Honeycomb 29

Honeycomb 29

I

ice cream *see also* parfait

Jasmine tea ice cream 174

Orange blossom ice-cream sandwich
    with lime curd 58–61

Porcini ice cream 157
   Strawberries & cream 96–99
Individual pavlovas 44–53
Italian meringue 87

J

jackfruit 198
   Bali sunrise 134–138
jam: Lemon jam 29
jasmine tea
   Opera 120–124
   White noise 174–179
Javanese long peppers 198
   Purple 186–191
jelly
   Berry consommé jelly 70,100
   Blueberry jelly 196
   Coffee jelly 78, 88
   Lime jelly 196
   Lychee jelly 99
   Passionfruit & pineapple jelly 138
   Raspberry consommé veil 182
   Rosewater jelly 95
   Strawberry gum jelly 176
   Verjuice jelly 62
   Yuzu jelly 80
Joconde 123

K

Kahlúa liqueur
   A slice of Irish Cream 74–78
   Tiramisu jar 88–91
King, Grant 168
kirsch: Blackforest jar 100–104
KOI Dessert Bar 8, 9, 70, 88, 130, 140
konjac powder 198

L

lava cake: Chocolate lava s'mores 84–87
lemongrass: Strawberries & cream 96–99
lemons
   Citrus meringue tart 36–39
   Lemon jam 29
limes
   Crème fraîche & lime chantilly 57
   Onyx 168–173
   Orange blossom ice-cream sandwich
      with lime curd 58–61

Passion berry cheesecake slice
   194–197
   Rum ba-banana & pineapple 54–57
lychees
   Mr Grey 80–83
   Strawberries & cream 96–99
   Watermelon jar 70–73

M

Magic mushrooms 154–159
maltodextrin 198
mango: Tropical panna cotta jar
   106–109
mascarpone cheese
   A slice of Irish Cream 74–78
   Tiramisu jar 88–91
   Vin & grapes 62
MasterChef 9, 174
matcha powder 198
   Matcha & yuzu ganache tart 34
   Moss 140–145
   Onyx 168–173
Matcha & yuzu ganache tart 34
meringue
   Bergamot & pink pepper
      meringue 180–183
   Cassis meringue 186
   Citrus meringue tart 36–39
   Individual pavlovas 44–53
   Italian meringue 84–87
Milk ice cream 99
Mille-tuile 110–113
Monkey's Corner 9
Moss 140–145
mousse
   Baileys mousse 77
   Chardonnay mousse 62
   Cheesecake mousse 194
   Chocolate mousse 26
   Coconut jackfruit mousse 134
   Coffee mousse 124
   Espresso mousse 130
   Pistachio monte 140
   Tiramisu mousse 91
Mr Grey 80–83
mushrooms: Magic mushrooms 154–159

N

Nomtella 130–133

O

oakwood chips 198
   Sitting in the forest 162–167
Onyx 168–173
Opera 120–124
Orange blossom ice-cream sandwich
   with lime curd 58–61
oranges: Citrus meringue tart 36–39

P

palm sugar 198
   Palm sugar sand 138
pandan extract 198
   Pandan gel 134
panna cotta
   Elderflower & vanilla panna
      cotta 96
   Tropical panna cotta jar 106–109
parfait
   Cassis parfait 189
   Coconut frozen parfait 174
   Orange blossom & vanilla
      parfait 58
Paris-Brest 43
Passion berry cheesecake slice 194–197
passionfruit
   Bali sunrise 134–138
   Passion berry cheesecake slice
      194–197
   Sitting in the forest 162–167
   Tropical panna cotta jar 106–109
pastry
   Chocolate choux 40–43
   Coffee tart shell 114
   French Earl Grey tart shell 36, 92
   Matcha tart shell 34
pavlovas
   Boozy berry pavlovas 52
   Cherry & coconut pavlovas 47
   Cinnamon pavlovas 48
   Individual pavlovas 44–53
   Spiced apple pavlovas 48–51
peanuts: The ultimate praline tart
   114–18
Pear & yuzu 150–152
pebbles: Strawberry pebbles 177
pectin NH powder 198
pepper: Red veil 180–183
Perfecta (50) 198

pineapple
Bali sunrise 134–138
Rum ba-banana & pineapple
54–57
Tropical panna cotta jar 106–109
pistachios
Brownie 18
Moss 140–145
pistachio paste 198
porcini powder 198
Magic mushrooms 154–159
praline paste 198
Peanut & hazelnut praline
paste 117
A slice of Irish cream 74–78
Tiramisu jar 88–91
Purple 186–191

R

Ramsay, Gordon 174
raspberries
Purple 186–191
Red veil 180–183
Ruby raspberry & rose tart 92–95
Watermelon jar 70–73
Red veil 180–183
rose petals 198
Ruby raspberry & rose tart 92–95
Watermelon jar 70–73
rosewater
Ruby raspberry & rose tart 92–95
Watermelon jar 70–73
ruby chocolate
Red veil 180–183
Ruby raspberry & rose tart 92–95
Ruby raspberry & rose tart 92–95
rum
Blackforest jar 100–104
Rum ba-banana & pineapple
54–57

S

sable
Almond sablé 61
Chocolate sablé crumbs 104
Sablé base 74, 120
Sablé crumble 73
sago pearls 198
Tropical panna cotta jar 106–109

sand: Palm sugar sand 138
Sitting in the forest 162–167
A slice of Irish Cream 74–78
soil
Chocolate soil 156, 166
Matcha soil 144
sorbet
Blackberry long pepper
sorbet 191
Raspberry hibiscus sorbet 183
Spiced apple pavlovas 48–51
sponge cake *see* cakes
strawberries
Boozy berry pavlovas 52
Mr Grey 80–83
Purple 186–191
Red veil 180–183
Ruby raspberry & rose tart
92–95
Strawberries & cream 96–99
Watermelon jar 70–73
White noise 174–179
strawberry gum powder 198
White noise 174–179

T

tarts
Citrus meringue tart 36–39
Matcha & yuzu ganache tart 34
Ruby raspberry & rose tart
92–95
The ultimate praline tart 114–18
tea
Citrus meringue tart 36–39
Mr Grey 80, 83
Opera 120–124
Red veil 180–183
White noise 174–179
Tiramisu jar 88–91
tree: Chocolate tree 165
Trimoline 198
Tropical panna cotta jar 106–109
tuiles
Charcoal tuiles 171
Dark brown sugar tuile 110

U

The ultimate praline tart 114–18
umeshu liqueur: Purple 186–191

V

vanilla
Mille-tuile 110–113
Spiced apple pavlovas 48–51
verjuice 198
Vin & grapes 62
Vin & grapes 62

W

Watermelon jar 70–73
whisky
An apple a day 146–149
Boozy berry pavlovas 52
white chocolate 10
An apple a day 146–149
Bali sunrise 134–138
Citrus meringue tart 36–39
Magic mushrooms 154–159
Matcha & yuzu ganache tart 34
Mille-tuile 110–113
Moss 140–145
Mr Grey 80–83
Nomtella 130–133
Onyx 168–173
Opera 120–124
Orange blossom ice-cream sandwich
with lime curd 58–61
Passion berry cheesecake slice 194–197
Pear & yuzu 150–152
Purple 186–191
Red veil 180–183
Ruby raspberry & rose tart 92–95
Sitting in the forest 162–167
Spiced apple pavlovas 48–51
Vin & grapes 62
White noise 174–179
White noise 174–179
wine
Ruby raspberry & rose tart 92–95
Vin & grapes 62

Y

yoghurt: White noise 174–179
yuzu juice 198
An apple a day 146–149
Matcha & yuzu ganache tart 34
Mr Grey 80–83
Pear & yuzu 150–152

ACKNOWLEDGEMENTS

It's been a lifelong dream of mine to write a cookbook. I am humbled and grateful to those who are behind making this dream finally come true. I've been very fortunate to have been surrounded by amazingly talented, creative and hard-working individuals who have worked with me on this book. It has made me enjoy every part of the journey, the process and the creativity, and inspired me to grow and reminded me once again why I love what I do.

Thank you, God, for giving me the strength and for the gift of creativity with which you have blessed my life, and for allowing me to be inspired by those around me and for allowing me to inspire others in the world of food.

To my Mum (Ike) and my brother Ronald — you've always got my back, through thick and thin, as well as allowing me to channel my creativity while you lead the business during my absence. Most importantly, you have inspired me and allowed me to utilise your creativity in this book — this book is as much yours as it is mine. My creativity would be nothing without both of you.

To the team at KOI Dessert Bar — Evan F, Elisha E and Felicity G, for helping me with the research and development of the recipes and looking after the rest of the kitchen team so that I can continue to focus and create. Elisha E, thank you for assisting me on shoot days — it has been an incredible help.

To Sharon F and Stephanie S — you have both created this opportunity for me to get my foot in the door. Despite being turned away a couple of times by other publishers, you both kept looking for the right opportunity for this to finally come true.

To Jeremy S and Amy J — for being incredible with your eye for detail, work and creativity, which allowed me to showcase my food in a new light. It was such a pleasure to be with you both on shoot days. It made me fall in love with food again and again, through the details of the photos with every shot.

To Jane M, Kristy A, Justin W, Emily O and Justine H — thank you all for making every stage of writing, editing and designing this book as low-stress as possible, and also for making it an enjoyable process. Also, of course, for giving me this opportunity and for the excitement of making this book come to life.

To my friends — thank you, potatoes, for always having my back, believing in me and supporting me through all the ups and downs of my life, and thank you to those who have been so encouraging of my work. You all inspire me to grow and I am forever grateful for that.

To July D and Chelia D — thank you both for inspiring and encouraging me. You've both supported me through many parts of my life and have influenced me and the recipes in this book. •

Published in 2021 by Murdoch Books, an imprint of Allen & Unwin

Murdoch Books Australia
83 Alexander Street
Crows Nest NSW 2065
Phone: +61 (0)2 8425 0100
murdochbooks.com.au
info@murdochbooks.com.au

Murdoch Books UK
Ormond House, 26–27 Boswell Street
London WC1N 3JZ
Phone: +44 (0) 20 8785 5995
murdochbooks.co.uk
info@murdochbooks.co.uk

For corporate orders and custom publishing, contact our business development team at
salesenquiries@murdochbooks.com.au

Publisher: Jane Morrow
Editorial Manager: Justin Wolfers
Design Manager: Kristy Allen
Designer: Emily O'Neill
Editor: Justine Harding
Photographer: Jeremy Simons
Stylist: Aimee Jones
Production Director: Lou Playfair

Text © Reynold Poernomo 2021
The moral right of the author has been asserted.
Design © Murdoch Books 2021
Photography © Jeremy Simons 2021
Photography page 8 © Tery Gunata

ISBN 978 1 92235 163 0 Australia
ISBN 978 1 91166 836 7 UK

A catalogue record for this
book is available from the
National Library of Australia

A catalogue record for this book is available from
the British Library

Colour reproduction by Splitting Image
Colour Studio Pty Ltd, Clayton, Victoria
Printed by 1010 Printing International Limited,
China

OVEN GUIDE: You may find cooking times vary
depending on the oven you are using. This book
uses fan-forced oven temperatures. If your oven
doesn't have a fan-forced setting, increase the
oven temperature to about 20°C (40°F) higher
than indicated in the recipe. The microwave used
in this book is 800W.

TABLESPOON MEASURES: We have used 20 ml
(4 teaspoon) tablespoon measures. If you are
using a 15 ml (3 teaspoon) tablespoon add an
extra teaspoon of the ingredient for each
tablespoon specified.

10 9 8 7 6 5 4